SAMPLING S~~~~~
Old country recipes
and
remedies

JUDY MOORE

Illustrations by Helen Fenton

S.B. Publications

By the same author
The Bloomsbury Trail in Sussex

For Euly, a far better cook than her mother

First published in 1996 by S B Publications
c/o 19 Grove Road, Seaford, East Sussex BN25 1TP

© Copyright 1996 Judy Moore

No part of this publication may be reproduced, stored in a retrieval system,
or transmitted in any form or by any means, electronic, mechanical,
photocopying, recording or otherwise, without the prior permission
of the publisher and copyright owner.

ISBN 1 85770 098 8

Typeset by CGB Lewes and printed by Island Press Ltd.

SAMPLING SUSSEX

Contents

Cover Illustration: Firle Beacon in High Summer
(Reproduced by kind permission of Susan Jackman; © Copyright Jackman Cards and Prints)

SOURCES AND BIBLIOGRAPHY

Many of the recipes in this book have been saved for posterity by the work of a number of Sussex people in the 1930s who researched and transcribed old receipts. Mrs M K Samuelson, secretary of the Sussex branch of the English Folk Cookery Association, compiled a *Sussex Recipe Book* in 1937 with the help of members of the public, who submitted their old family recipes.

She was assisted by Sussex historian, Edward Shoosmith, who was born at Claverham Manor House, Arlington, in the 1860s. He transcribed for her a hand written, sheepskin bound volume entitled *Booke of Receipts,* begun by Philadelphia Shoebridge in 1708 when she was twenty six years of age.

Philadelphia married Henry Miller of Birghill when she was forty-nine, died a year later, and is buried in the churchyard at Chiddingly. Shoosmith also contributed many of his own family recipes both to Mrs Samuelson's book and to a series on Sussex cookery in the *Sussex County Magazine.*

In the same decade Marcus Woodward wrote *The Mistress of Stantons Farm,* an account of the extraordinary life of Susannah Stacey. She was a farmer's wife at East Chiltington who attained considerable local fame in the last century as a herbalist, wise woman and a creative cook. Many of her receipts are preserved in the book.

Other sources include the books of William Verral, innkeeper and chef at The White Hart in Lewes in the eighteenth century; various manuscripts compiled by housewives and housekeepers in the seventeenth, eighteenth and nineteenth centuries, among them Mary Bays, Barbara Young, Ann Lord and Mrs J Gould; and a manuscript household book discovered in the library of Edward, Duke of Norfolk at Arundel Castle. Some of its receipts, in the original spelling, were published in the *Sussex County Magazine* in the 1930s.

Among other books consulted are:

A Boke of Kokery, Lewes Priory Trust.

A Little Place in the Country by Marjorie Hessell Tiltman, Hodder and Stoughton, 1944.

A New System of Cookery by William Verral, 1759 (reprinted as *William Verral's Cookery Book*, Southover Press, 1988).

A Sussex Farmer by William Wood, Jonathan Cape, 1938.

A Sussex Life, The Memories of Gilbert Sargent, edited Dave Arthur, Barrie and Jenkins, 1989.

By Weald and Down by A A Evans, Methuen, 1939.

Cottage Pie by Marjorie Hessell Tiltman, Hodder and Stoughton, 1940.

County Recipes of Old England compiled by Helen Edden.

Food from Firle by Lady Gage, 1978.

Good Things in England, edited by Florence White, Jonathan Cape, 1932.

Kitchen Fugue by Sheila Kaye-Smith, Cassell, 1945.

Memories of Old Sussex by Lillian Candlin, Countryside Books, 1987.

Sussex County Magazine 1927-1956.

Sussex Recipe Book, compiled by M K Samuelson, Country Life, 1937.

The Folklore of Sussex by Jacqueline Simpson, Batsford, 1973.

The Highways and Byways of Sussex by E V Lucas, Macmillan, 1928.

The Mistress of Stantons Farm by Marcus Woodward, Heath Cranton, 1938.

Twenty Centuries in Sedlescombe by Beryl Lucy, Regency Press, 1978.

Village at War by Anthony Armstrong, Collins, 1941.

We Keep Going by Anthony Armstrong, Collins, 1946.

William Verral's Complete System of Cookery, 1759 (reprinted as *A Cooks Paradise,* Sylvan Press, 1948).

SUSSEX PARSLEY

Unless I plants our parsley bed
I'll have wi' you no truck,
Ses I to him, for she, I said,
Can give or take our luck.
You, lad, may dig and hoe and weed
The taters in their rows.
But women-folk sow parsley seed,
As all in Sussex knows.

For parsley has a power, lad,
That's old as histories.
'Twas guv her as a dower, lad,
By Downland pharisees;
And we'll grow rich or come to need
According whether frowns
Or smiles she gives. That's true indeed
As stand the Sussex Downs.

Ethel Talbot

INTRODUCTION

V AST, dense Wealden forests, and heavy clay mud that made tracks impassable for many months of the year combined to isolate old Sussex from its neighbours. Out of touch, and out of step, the people depended for their food on what they could grow and breed and the catches from river and sea.

'Why is it that the oxen, the swine, the women, and all other animals are so long-legged in Sussex?' Dr John Burton inquired in *Iter Sussexiense,* published in 1751. 'May it be from the difficulty of pulling the feet out of so much mud by the strength of the ankle that the muscles get stretched, as it were, and the bones lengthened?'

There is an apocryphal story illustrating the state of the roads in the eighteenth century. A traveller came upon a hat lying in the mud. When he lifted the hat he found a man beneath it. When asked if he required assistance, the buried man said: 'Never mind me, look to my horse'. When excavated the horse was found to be feeding from a cartload of hay lost the previous day.

Sussex is a fertile county, a fact which encouraged the invading Romans to cultivate cherries, apples and vines. The Saxons, who came next, were hearty eaters with a liking for mutton, beef and milk puddings made with cereals and honey. Younger, more tender meat such as veal and lamb was preferred by the Normans, who came ashore at Pevensey in 1066.

Although cut off from the rest of England, inland, Sussex was open to the sea and a two way trade exporting wool and importing wine, brandy and spices – especially valued for disguising rotting meats – flourished. Dried fruits came from Portugal and the Levant, and a greater variety of medicinal herbs became available when the monks established their herb gardens in the eleventh and twelfth centuries.

Sheila Kaye-Smith, a Sussex novelist with an intimate knowledge of the county and thus one who should have known better, claimed that Sussex had 'no historic dishes or ways of eating such as are the pride of other parts of England'.

The local cattle, she said, were 'notoriously poor milkers . . . nor have we local cheeses, as in the west, or local cakes and pies as in the north . . . of course there is South Down mutton, famous throughout the world; but our Sussex women have no proud ways of cooking it.

'The fact is that the old-time Sussex man ate what he could get and his wife cooked it as best she could over a few sticks. She had no facilities and probably no energy for making pasties or plum cakes, for puddings or clotted cream, for scones or buns or teabread.'

She could not have been more wrong – probably because she knew absolutely nothing about cooking. Until she became servantless during the Second World War she had never even made herself a cup of tea.

Sussex cookery, before cans and packaging, before freezers, microwave ovens and supermarkets, was unique, inventive, delicious and sustaining.

Yorkshire may have its celebrated but tasteless, air-filled batter pudding, Lancashire its watery hot pot, Devonshire its clotted cream and scones. Sussex, by contrast, has its glorious pond pudding, its drip pudding, plum heavies and cracklings.

Suet puddings, sweet and savoury, were the staff of life of both affluent and humble homes, often served daily. Do not go to Sussex, was once the advice, or they will turn you into a pudding.

What puddings there were, too – beef puddings and pork puddings, plum puddings and herb puddings, puddings light as a feather stuffed with fish, with fruit, with syrup.

Seal, swan, goose, crane, heron and peacock, beef and mutton were served in the homes of the rich, pork more often in poorer households. 'Pygges, specially some pygges, is nutrytyve,' wrote Cuckfield born Andrew Boorde, the sixteenth century monk who left

8

the cloisters to study medicine. 'A yonge fatte pygge in physicke is singularly praysed, if it be well ordered in the rostynge.'

The famous four (or seven, or fourteen) Good Things of Sussex have been variously attributed to Izaak Walton, the Rev Thomas Fuller and Arthur Becket. In fact it was Walton who first identified the 'good things' in *The Compleat Angler,* his pocketbook for fishermen published in 1653.

His four were 'a Shelsey Cockle, a Chichester Lobster, an Arundel Mullet and an Amerley Trout'. Nine years later Fuller repeated these four in *The Worthies of England,* in a section headed Natural Commodities.

Then came Francis Grose, an antiquary and an early travel writer, who made a tour of Sussex in 1777. In his *Provincial Glossary* he listed: 'A Chichester lobster, a Selsey cockle, an Arundel mullett, a Pulborough eel, an Amberley trout, a Rye herring, a Bourne wheat ear. These are all the best of their kind, at least of any that are taken in this county.'

These seven good things were added to again by Admiral BM Chambers, in 1936. His additions were a saddle of Southdown mutton, a Patching truffle pie, Goring figs, Downland mushrooms, Dungeness honey, Worthing grapes and tomatoes.

It was perhaps as well that the admiral chose a career at sea since his geography was none too accurate. Dungeness is in Kent, but close enough to the border for Kentish bees to gather their nectar in Sussex. As for Arthur Beckett – he appears to have gathered all these good things together to form his own list.

So, the ingredients were all to hand for those with the means, fish and fowl, meat and game, fruit, cereals and vegetables. The creation of memorable dishes was not so easy, though, when all that cooks had available were spits and bottle jacks, dutch ovens, gridirons and iron stew pots.

A built in brick oven, where one was provided, was for bread, pies, tarts and cakes. Oven roasting of meat dates from around 1840 when the first ranges became available. Before that time meat was

A two oven range of the 1890s

roasted on a spit before an open fire. The fat was preserved by covering it with paper tied with fine twine, never pins or skewers as they were 'taps' that let out the juices. A dripping pan was placed to catch the juices to use for gravy. Cooks had to be expert judges of timing not to burn the meat, and they had to gauge the heat of the fire to prevent it from becoming tough.

Meat could also be broiled on a gridiron over a fire. The gridiron was a frame supported on four legs, with concave bars terminating in a trough to catch the gravy and keep the fat from dropping into the fire. There was also a vertical gridiron in which steaks or chops were sandwiched between two sets of bars. This was hung over the fire and had a tray to collect fat and juices.

Many dined extremely well. Thomas Turner, the shopkeeper, schoolteacher and undertaker of East Hoathly in the mid eighteenth century, records in his diary the consumption of daily meals that today would require a healthy income as well as a healthy constitution.

He would, for instance, dine at midday on two roasted ducks, a piece of bacon, a leg of mutton, cauliflowers and carrots, with a boiled currant pond pudding, and perhaps have for his supper a piece of cold roast beef, cold giblet pasty, some cold roast goose, neat's tongues, apple pasty and bread and cheese.

Like Turner, many Sussex people were great trenchermen, both gourmands and gourmets, inordinately fond of their 'puddin and tame' – the Saxon phrase for food and drink.

Here are some of the receipts used over the centuries, many as they were originally written, complete with archaic spelling. Quite a number, with a little adjustment of quantities, are as good today as ever they were. Others would be too expensive, or not for present day palates – and one or two are downright disgusting.

Here also are remedies and recipes for healing and curing all manner of ills including even cancer and the plague. Few can be recommended and a number should definitely carry a government health warning.

SOUPS AND SAUCES

OLD time cooks in Sussex could not reach for a stock cube, a packet or frozen sachet of sauce, a jar of gravy browning; they had to start from scratch. The basis for their soups, sauces and gravies could be as simple as a few boiled bones with a handful of herbs or as complicated as William Verral's broth and cullis.

Verral, keeper of The White Hart, Lewes, in the eighteenth century, was trained in the French art of cooking and took great pains both in the preparation of his dishes and in the scrupulous cleanliness of his kitchen. His broth, a basis for soups and gravies, and his cullis, a basic brown sauce, are among the ingredients of a number of recipes in this book.

Modern substitutes may, of course, be used but those who wish to recreate an authentic eighteenth century dish should follow the Verral recipes, reducing the quantities to manageable and affordable proportions. Both the broth and the cullis can be frozen in ice trays or small containers and stored in the freezer until needed.

Verral's Broth

In a pot that holds three or four gallons place a leg or shin of beef (eight to ten pounds) of the lean part which, in London, is called the mouse-buttock, and a knuckle of veal. Fill the pot with water and place it on the heat, skimming as necessary, adding a little salt which causes the skim to rise. Simmer, season with ten to twelve large onions, eight to ten carrots, three or four turnips, a parsnip, two or three leeks, a bundle of celery, a few cloves, a blade or two of mace and whole white pepper. Boil until the meat is tender – no more for to boil it to rags (as is the common practice) makes the broth thick and grouty, and spoils the pleasing aspect of all your dinner, and hurts the meat that thousands of families would leap mast-high at. Strain it through a lawn sieve into a clean earthen pan, skim off the fat.

Verral's Cullis

Take a stewpan that will hold about four quarts, put a thin slice or two of bacon at the bottom, about two pounds of veal, a piece of ham, three or four carrots, onions and parsley, with a head or two of celery. Pour in about a pint of your broth (see previous recipe), cover it close, and let it go gently on upon a slow stove for an hour. When it comes to be almost dry watch it narrowly, so as to bring it to a nice brown, fill it up with broth and let it boil softly about half an hour. Take about half a pound of fresh butter, melt it, three or four large spoonfuls of fine flour, and rub over a stove till it is a fine yellowish or light brown colour, pour it into your gravy, take the roots out, and pass it through your sieve. Be sure great care is taken on this, for on it the goodness and beauty of all the rest depends.

Egg Soup

Break the yolks of two eggs into a dish with a piece of butter as big as an egg. Take a tea-kettle of boiling water in one hand, and a spoon in the other; pour in about a quart by degrees, stir it all the time, till the eggs are well mixed and the butter melted; then pour it into a saucepan, and continue stirring it till it begins to simmer. Take it off the fire and pour it between two vessels, out of one into another, till it is quite smooth, and has a great froth on it. Set it on the fire again, and keep stirring it till it is quite hot; then put it into the soup dish, and send it to table hot.   *Susannah Stacey*

Another type of egg soup comes from William Verral, who said about it: 'This may seem to be but a simple thing to place among these high matters; but I never see it come from table without a terrible wound in it. If it has but the approbation of few it will pay very well for the room it takes up here.'

Soup for Supper

To a quart of good new milk put a pint of cream, a bit of lemon peel, a laurel leaf or two, and a stick of cinnamon, and a few coriander seeds, and some good sugar; boil it for a few minutes, and set off to cool; blanch two ounces of sweet almonds, with two or three bitter ones, pound them with a drop of water to a paste, and stir them in your milk, rub it through a sieve, pour it back into your stewpan and make it just boiling. Provide the yolks of about ten eggs, and pour in. Beat nice and smooth, stir it upon your stove carefully for a minute or two, and it is ready to serve to table, putting on it some rusks or toasts of French bread.

13

There are early examples of today's instant soups in the Arundel manuscript. The one for Solid Soup has similarities to a Portable Soup given in *An Improved System of Domestic Economy, containing Eight Hundred Valuable Receipts,* published in 1827. The Portable Soup involved taking 'a leg of beef, scrag of mutton, a knuckle of veal, a set of calf's feet and three gallons of water'. This was boiled for several days until it reached the consistency of glue, when it was poured into teacups to set. Subsequently the hard substance was heated and diluted to form soup or stock. The Arundel 'instant soup' recipe is more detailed.

Lady Wager's Receipt for Solid Soup

Take a Leg of veal or any other young meat (because old will not jelly) cut of all the fatt & make strong broth after the Common way, this broth pour into a wide flat silver Bason & let it simmer over an even charcoal fire not too hot till more than halfe is boiled away skimming it often to keep it from burning. Then remove it from ye fire & sett it over boiling water which is an evener heat & not so apt to burn ye broth to ye vessel. Let it evaporate stiring it often till it becoms when cold a substance as hard as glue. This dry before ye fire & will keep years, provided you hinder any moisture from coming to it. When you would use the broth you have no more to doe than to disolve a Little of it in boiling water puting in more or Less according to ye strength you would have ye soup off & will be as good as can be made. Put ye watter over a stove & boilen ye soup over ye water with neither salt nor spice in it for that you season when you make your soup. It looks just like hard dry glue.

Pease Soup

Boyle a piece of Bacon in ye Pot with ye Pease, & when they are Boyled enough pour as much as you have occasion for through a cullender, do not braid ye Pease least they make it too thick. Put ye liquor into ye stew pan with about half a pint of gravy or strong broth, a little mace, whole pepper & one anchovy if ye Bacon has not made it to salt before, then burn some Butter which must be done by strowing in ye flower by Little & Little to keep it from runing till it looks brown, put that into ye soop. Just before you send it in, throw in some shred spinage, fry piece of Bread cut in dice & put into it.

To Make a Soop

Take a neck of mutton & three chickens & boyle them in 8 quarts of water till they consume to two quarts, then strain it & season it with whole peper, mace & a nutmeg & two or three onions. Let it boyle a little tender then take out the spice and put in two or three handfulls of spinage, as much sorrell as much letticce & one pound of butter. Let it boyle a quarter of an hour & keep it stirring & serve it up with a boyld chicken in the middle.

Sorrel Soup

Peel and chop an onion and cook it in a tablespoon of oil until soft. Add 12 large sorrel leaves and continue cooking gently until the sorrel is soft and limp. Add two and a half pints of light stock, bring to the boil, add one pound of peas and simmer for 15 minutes. Puree and add salt, pepper and the grated peel of one lemon.

Potage Meagre

Charge a Pot with a Galon of fair water, when it boyls Scum it, & put in some Spinage, Lettice, Sellery, Endive, some Onions minced; put in a pound of Butter, some toasts of French bread; add a blade of large Mace, a little Pepper & Salt, a fagot of sweet herbs; let these stew gently a quarter of an hour; then put in some Vermecelli & let it boyl till you see it swelled to the height; then dish it with poached Eggs.

Philadelphia Shoebridge

Green Leaf Soup

Chop an onion and a few cloves of garlic and fry in two ounces of butter. Add two pints of water, a bacon knuckle or ham bone and a handful of the young leaves of dandelion, violets, nettle tops and watercress. Simmer for at least an hour. Mix one and a half ounces of flour with a little water, add some of the soup then add to the soup while stirring. Heat again and serve with chopped hard boiled egg

Green Pea Soup

Take a Nuckell of a Scragg of Veal. Boil it with a quart of Green Peas, two or three Onions, a Sprigg of Time, a little whole pepper. When it is boiled Strain it through a Cullender and pulp the peas through it into a Stewpan. When it is boild, put in a pint of young peas, tops of green Mint, lett them Boil tender, then put in a piece of Butter, Flower and Season it to your tast. You must make it of a proper Green with juice of Spinnage.

Family Cullis

Take a piece of butter rolled in flour, stir it in your stewpan till the flour is of a fine yellow colour; then put in some stock, a glass of white wine, a bundle of parsley, thyme, laurel and sweet basil, two cloves, some nutmeg or mace, a few mushrooms, pepper and salt. Let it stew an hour over a slow fire, then skim all the fat clean off, and strain it through a lawn sieve.
Susannah Stacey

Sorrel Sauce

Wash, squeeze and chop fine plenty of sorrel, and put it into a stewpan with a bit of fresh butter; stew it till the liquor is nearly wasted, and add a little strong cullis. The sauce must be of a good thickness.
Susannah Stacey

To Make a Green Sauce

Take a good handful of sorrel and pound it small, with a little grated bread, and two hard eggs, with ye pap of a boyld Pippen (apple), beat all these well together with a littel Vinegar, and sweeten it with Sugar, and put it into plates. This is proper for a leg of Veal and bacon.

Cucumber Sauce

Peel the cucumbers, and cut them into quarters, take out all the seed, cut each quarter into three pieces, pare them round, peel as many small onions as pieces of cucumber; let them lie for two hours in some vinegar and water, pepper and salt them; pour off the vinegar and water and put as much stock as will just cover them; boil them down to a glaze; add as much cullis as you think proper; let it boil for a few minutes, squeeze a lemon, and put in a little sugar.
Susannah Stacey

Piquant Sauce

Put two sliced onions, with a piece of butter, into a stewpan; a carrot, parsnip, a turnip, a little thyme, sorrel, basil, two cloves, two shallots, a clove of garlic, and some parsley; turn it over the fire till well coloured; then shake in a little flour, and moisten it with some stock, and a spoonful of vinegar. Let it boil gently a few minutes, then skim and strain it through a sieve; season with salt and pepper.

Aspic Sauce

Infuse chervil, tarragon, burnet, garden cress, and mint into a little cullis for half an hour; then strain it and add a spoonful of garlic vinegar, with a little pepper and salt.

Sauce for Fish

Take a quarte of a pint of Clarrat & a good deal of shread Lemon with a little of the pill (peel), two blades of mace & sliced nuttmeg, an anchovy or two, half a spoonfull of whole peper, a sprig of winter savory & tyme, put all these into a sauce pan and boyle it over Coals till it be half shrunk in or better, then take out yr time & savory & shake it up with butter; if you please you may beat ye yolk of an egg & put into it twill thicken the sauce. When you boyle ye fish cover it with watter, put in a Little vinegar, half a handfull of salt, a spoonfull of whole pepper, a little mace & a bundle of tyme & winter savory, a Little lemon pill. Lett the water boyle before ye fish goes in.

Arundel ms

Sauce for Stewed or Boyld Fish

Take half a pint of white wine, with half a pint of gravy or strong broth and put to it 3 or 4 shalots, a Nutmeg cut into slices, a bunche of sweet herbs, a little lemon pill (peel), and 3 or 4 anchovies, and let this boyl a quarter of an hour; then put to it ye yolks of 3 or 4 eggs well beaten, shake it well together till it begins to thick, and put to a ladlefull or 2 of drawn butter that is melted, thick; ye fish being draind, from ye water and in ye dish, you may put some smal fryd-fish on ye top, some stewed Olives, prawns, or shrimps being stewed with ye oysters, (dipt in butter and fryd), with a few sippets of white bread all over it, and garnish it with sliced limon, ye brim of ye dish red cabbage, parsly, flower and hard eggs, being mixt with green herbs.

Philadelphia Shoebridge

Mushroom Catsup

Take fresh gathered full grown mushrooms; put a layer of these at the bottom of a deep fireproof pot, sprinkle them with salt, then another layer of mushrooms and then more salt and so on, until your pot is full. Let it remain two or three hours, then pound the mushrooms in a mortar or crush them with your hands. Let them remain for a couple of days, mashing and stirring them well each day. Then put them into a stone jar and to each quart add an ounce and a half of whole pepper, and half an ounce of allspice; cover the jar closely and set it in a stew pan of boiling water and keep it boiling for two hours at least. Strain through a hair sieve and boil the liquid gently for another half hour; then bottle and cork very securely.

M K Samuelson

Walnute Catchup

Take two hundred of wallnuts when they are full grown & so soft as you may put a pin through them, beat them very small in a marble morter & steep them a fortnight in vinegar covered over then strain them off and boyle up ye Liquor & skim it well then put in half an ounce of mace & a quarter of an ounce of cloves, a quarter of an ounce of nuttmegs & a trace or two of Ginger and half an ounce of whole pepper & salt to your test. This quantity of spice is a nuff for two Quarts of Liquor, when tis cold Bottle it up for your use. It will keep two or three years.
Arundel ms

Bread Sauce with Saffron

Put a good-sized white onion peeled and cut into quarters into a saucepan; add about a dozen black peppercorns, three cloves, a small blade of mace, a pinch of grated nutmeg, and a saltspoonful of salt. Pour over these ingredients a little more than half a pint of milk. Place the saucepan over a very low fire or tiny gas-flame. Remove the saucepan as soon as the surface of the milk looks frothy; let it cool a little and replace, continuing to do this several times until the onion is fairly soft. Now add six grains of saffron obtained from a chemist, and, if necessary, some extra milk to make good the loss by evaporation. Boil up once more and strain the milk through a piece of muslin into a bowl, and add to it, very gradually spoonful by spoonful, the stale breadcrumbs you have already prepared, until the right consistency has been attained. Then heat the sauce up again as already described, adding at the last moment before serving a tablespoonful of cream. Suitable for use with all roast fowl, pheasant, partridge and grouse.
Edward Shoosmith 1936

Salad Sauce

Take the hard yolks of two eggs, a dessertspoonful of grated Parmesan cheese, a little mustard, a dessertspoonful of tarragon vinegar, and a spoonful of ketchup (see mushroom catsup). When well incorporated, add four spoonfuls of salad oil, and one of elder vinegar. Beat it so as to incorporate the oil with the other ingredients.
Susannah Stacey

PIGS BE NUTRYTIVE

SUSSEX is pig-shaped, with the snout at Rye, the rear at Uppark and the legs at Selsey Bill and Beachy Head. Nor is the county's shape its only porcine attribute; Sussex people were, before the breed was diluted by 'furriners', pig-headed folk who 'wun't be druv'.

Could this have been because, over many centuries, they ate more pig than any other meat? From Saxon days Sussex sustained huge numbers of swine that subsisted almost entirely on acorns, beech-mast and fruits of the woodlands. The value of the woods, from forest to small coppices, was reckoned in the Domesday Book by pannage – the number of swine it sustained.

Maude Robinson, who grew up on a farm at Saddlescombe near the Devil's Dyke in the mid nineteenth century, wrote that there was little fresh meat for either master or man, with the exception of pig.

Most country people kept a pig in the back garden. Those who could afford it bought two piglets in the spring, one for their own larders, the other to fatten and sell. A piglet was bought for a few pence, rising to a few shillings in Victoria's time, and was fed on kitchen and garden scraps and skimmed milk, until the last few weeks of its life when it was fattened, to between twenty and thirty stones, with barley or oatmeal. Pig meat was the term for fresh meat, and pork for salted pig meat.

The pig was known to country people as 'the gentleman who pays the rent'. The gentleman's carcase provided food for the family and cash when parts were sold, so helping to pay the rent.

The pig was a pampered pet, but not for sentimental reasons. Maude Robinson remembered hearing discontented squeals from a pig that stood by a full trough and looked appealingly at its mistress, who explained: 'Well, you see Miss, he ain't accustomed to cold suppers. I biles up everything for he and gives it to he warm but today I been out leasing and the fire's out, so his lordship has got to have it cold, and he don't like it.'

The pampering was in anticipation of succulent roast meat, crackling, brawn, meat puddings, bacon and fleed cakes.

The Rev WD Parish recalled, in his *Dictionary of the Sussex Dialect* (1875): 'A parishioner of mine once came to complain to me that her husband had threatened to ill-use her on account of two little pigs which she was hobbing-up; but as I found that his objection rested on the fact that she was hobbing-up the pigs so carefully that she insisted on taking them to bed with her, I declined to interfere'. Hobbing was the old country word for hand-rearing.

Every morsel from tail to snout was used. Hams were cured, bacon smoked and the chitterlings cleaned for sausage skins. The liver was fried, the fleed (inside fat) refined into lard, trotter pies were made, stews made from leftover offal and any scraps remaining were combined with dried fruit and made into scrap pie.

Small crisp cakes called crackings were baked. Haslet and sausages were made – the sausages being all meat with the addition of only pepper, salt and sage. Skirt was used to make meat puddings, blood for black puddings and the dripping, spread on bread, made a tasty breakfast. Even the skin was used, to make brawn. Nothing was wasted, not even the pig's manure which was spread on the garden to nourish the soil.

After the pig killing the hams were rubbed daily with salt and salt-petre for three weeks then hung in a wide chimney over a fire of juniper berries, wet straw and sawdust to be smoked. Some of the larger farms had smoking sheds where cottagers were allowed to hang their own bacon.

Neighbours who had helped feed a pig with 'peelings and wash' were rewarded at pig killing time with choice pieces of meat, or they received morsels in anticipation of returned favours when their pigs were killed.

The practice of keeping a pig in the back garden petered out at the end of the Victorian age, but was revived some forty years later when, during World War Two, the Ministry of Food urged larger households (where there was likely to be more in the way of table scraps) to consider taking on a pig.

There are pigs in unexpected places in Sussex. This one in its barrel formed the inn sign of the Runt in Tun at Heathfield, a pub which takes its name from the former parish of Runtington

Anthony Armstrong tells the tale of a neighbour of his in West Sussex who applied to the proper authorities for a young female pig so that there would be a plentiful supply of pork and bacon during the hostilities.

When the piglet arrived there were puppies in the household and the young porker grew to think that she, too, was a dog. She frol-icked with the pups and so often followed them when they went for their daily walk that the owner had to buy her a collar and lead. The pig learned to come to the whistle and was soon as much a part of the family as were the dogs. It was, of course, out of the question to eat her.

The man from the pig authority arrived and asked to see the pig, expecting to be taken to the sty. The owner whistled and Frances Bacon galloped up. All the official could suggest was that the owner contact a pig farmer and breed from Frances. Unfortunately, Frances considered herself a dog and her romance with a neighbouring boar was short lived when she spurned him out of trotter.

Bacon Pudding

Make a suet crust of six ounces of flour to three ounces of shredded suet and a pinch of salt. Roll it out thinly and spread with chopped bacon, onion, sage and pepper. Turn over as for a jam roly poly and tie in a cloth. Boil for two hours in an iron pot. Serve surrounded by rape greens (the tops of swede turnips) worked like spinach.

Pork Rind Brawn

Soak the pork rinds for twelve hours in salt water. Put them into a saucepan with enough cold water to cover them. Add black pepper, peppercorns, cloves, bay leaves and the bones of any joints you may have by you. Simmer for five or six hours till the rinds are all tender. Take out the rinds and chop up very fine. Strain the liquor. Put all back into the saucepan and bring to the boil. Pour into a mould and leave to get cold. It will set in a firm jelly.

Lillian Candlin, a recipe used by her grandmother

Sussex Brawn

Boil half a head of pig with half a pound of best English skirt, or gravy beef, a bunch of herbs tied up in muslin, well seasoned with pepper and salt and a small piece of mace for two and a half hours. Take out the bones, chop of the remainder and turn into moulds.

Ifield Vicarage Hogs Pudding

Cut one pound of pork flank into slices, put into hot water and boil for 45 minutes. Mix one teaspoon of baking powder, one pound of currants, and a pinch of spice with one and a half pounds of flour and one pound of diced lard. Add the meat. Fill sausage skins with the mixture, tie up in bunches, prick them with a fork and plunge the puddings into boiling water. Boil for one and a half hours, take out the puddings and hang them up to dry.

Sussex Hogs Pudding

Mix together the following: Flour 1lb, currants 10oz, pork fat chopped fine 11oz, allspice 2oz, moist sugar 2 handfuls, salt one-third of teaspoonful, nutmeg ditto. Slice into the basin nearly 2oz dripping (not any more). Pour over the whole boiling water enough to make a very stiff mixture. Shape into a roll pudding with a cloth round it and boil quite 4 hours or more. Turn out of cloth when quite cold or keep in cloth until required.

Mid Victorian family recipe book

Fifty or sixty years earlier hogs pudding contained no pig meat at all, only pig gut. The following recipe dates from around 1790.

Take three pounds of grated bread to four pounds of beef suet finely shred, two pounds of currants clean picked and washed, cloves, mace and cinnamon of each a quarter of an ounce finely beaten, a little salt, a pound and a half of sugar, a pint of sack, a quart of cream, a little rose-water, twenty eggs well beaten, but half the whites; mix all these well together, fill the guts half full, boil them a little and prick them as they boil to keep them from breaking the guts; take them up upon clean cloths, then lay them on your dish; or when you use them, boil them a few minutes again or eat them cold.

Lady Grace Pelham's Bloud Pudding

As soon as the bloud (collected after a pig killing) is well settled put in as much great Oatmeal, as you think will make it thick. When you goe to make the Puddings, have in readiness a good quantity of Pennyroyal, sweet Marjerom, a little Parsly & Thyme: let them be shred very small; have some Nutmeg, Cloves, Mace a little Pepper beat very small; have a good quantity of hogs Fat ready cut, & warm Milk as much as will make it of a good thickness; then put in the Herbs, Spice & Fat; Season it to your taste with Salt; then put in the yolks of Eggs proportionable to the quantity; let them be well beaten, & a little grated bread; then fill them (the bladders). Have everything ready when you goe to mix it.

Coger Cakes

1lb raw, thick, fat salt pork, 24oz flour, 4oz currants, 4oz sugar. Take a knife and scrape all the fat off the rind of the pork, then rub in the flour, add sugar and currants, and make into a dough. Roll out 2 inches thick and bake on a baking sheet for 30-45 minutes in a hot oven.

Coger cakes were also made without currants and formed into a cake of a convenient size to fit into a man's pocket for his midday meal.

Fleed Cakes

Cut up 12oz fleed into small pieces and rub it, and 2oz butter, into 1lb plain flour. Add a pinch of salt. Mix with water to a soft dough and turn out on to a floured board. Roll out thinly, three, four or more times. On each occasion work in more flour and butter (8oz flour and 6oz butter in total). It is important to get as much air into the dough as possible after each rolling by continually folding. Fold the dough and stand it aside in a cold place for at least 12 hours. Roll it out to quarter of an inch thick, cut into 5in rounds, lightly fold the rounds in half and again into quarters. Wash the tops with egg and stand in a cold place for 30 minutes before placing in a hot oven for 20–30 minutes.

Scrap Cakes

2lb fleed, 8oz flour, 4oz moist sugar, 8oz currants, 1oz candied lemon peel, ground allspice. Cut the fleed into small pieces and place these in a large dish in a hot oven to reduce. When the fleed has been reduced to small scraps floating on the surface of the oil remove from the oven and press the scraps flat under greaseproof paper. The oil solidifies to become lard. Put the scraps in a basin with flour and rub them well together. Add all the other ingredients, moisten with enough water to make a dough and roll it out thinly. Cut the dough into shapes and bake in a quick oven for 15–20 minutes.

Pork Pudding

Cut fresh pig meat into dice and layer it in a pudding basin with thinly sliced potatoes, sage and chopped onion until the basin is full. Cover with greaseproof paper and a pudding cloth and boil for at least one and a half hours. Serve with apple sauce.

Sussex Farmhouse Pate

Mince one pound of belly pork with half a pound of bacon pieces, half a pound of pig liver, a medium onion, two teaspoons chopped fresh herbs (parsley, sage, marjoram, thyme), one teaspoon mixed dried herbs, salt and pepper. Add four ounces of breadcrumbs to the mixture and press into a greased one pound loaf tin. Cover with greaseproof paper, place the tin in a second container filled with water to half way up the tin's side and cook in the centre of a medium oven for about one and three quarter hours. Weight the pate and leave it to cool.

PUDDINGS AND PIES

SUSSEX and suet are, or used to be before its residents became as health conscious as the rest of the country, synonymous. Just about everything could be steamed, boiled or baked inside a suet dough – fruits and vegetables, butter and sugar, meat, fish and poultry. A suet pudding in one form or another was eaten every day in many Sussex homes. Before cookers, or stoves as they used to be called, became standard kitchen fixtures, everyday cooking was done in a bread oven or a big iron pot suspended over an open fire.

The suet pudding was formed into a ball, or a sausage shape, wrapped tightly in cloth and plunged into boiling water in the pot, leaving room for nets of vegetables around it.

In large households, and on farms, where the unmarried labourers lived in, the pot was rarely big enough to hold enough puddings and the copper in which the weekly wash was done was used. This was a large container built into a brick support beneath which a fire was lit to boil the washing. However well the copper was scoured the puddings must always have tasted faintly of soap.

Popular savoury puddings were made with pork, onion and apple; pork sausagemeat; beef and kidney; bacon; rabbit and partridge. Swede, mashed with plenty of butter, pepper and salt, was the usual accompaniment.

In really poor households, when suet was not available, a pudding called Hard Dick was made by mixing flour, water and a pinch of salt. It was left in a warm place to set and was then boiled in a cloth. Labourers took a slice of Hard Dick to the fields for their midday meal with a piece of cheese and an onion.

The Rev WD Parish blamed Hard Dick, when eaten cold, for all the ills the flesh is heir to. 'It promotes a dyspeptic form of dissent which is unknown elsewhere,' he wrote. 'It aggravates every natural infirmity of temper by the promotion of chronic indigestion, and finally undermines the constitution. The first symptom of the decay of nature which a Sussex man describes is invariably that he can't get his pudding to set.'

Plumb pudding, or plumb pottage, was a starter, a between course appetiser and often a finisher too in well-to-do households. A typical recipe would consist of a leg or shin of beef, six penny loaves, five pounds of currants, five pounds of raisins, two pounds of prunes, spices, three pounds of sugar, two pints of claret, lemons and sago.

In 1797 a Cuckfield flax dresser wagered he could eat a square foot of plumb pudding in a fortnight. The *Sussex Weekly Advertiser,* a newspaper that knew a good human interest story when it saw one, sent along a reporter who recorded the events for posterity. He declared that a square foot of pudding, properly cooked, should weigh 42lb. The locals entered into the spirit of the curious undertaking and a great many bets were placed.

On January 9 the paper reported: 'The man who undertook to eat his way through 2 lbs more than a moiety of it on Wednesday last which was his seventh day's performance, ate 4 lbs at his first meal, but appeared rather crop-sick for the remainder of that day and the next. By way of science, he sometimes uses a great quantity of mustard with his pudding, and at other times, sops it with vinegar.'

And on January 16: 'The plum-pudding eater on the eighth day found his gormandizers jaws absolutely refusing to stir any longer in the service; in consequence of which he was reluctantly necessitated to give in!'

SAVOURY PUDDINGS

Drip Pudding

Make a plain suet pudding (eight ounces of flour, four ounces of suet), roll it in a floured cloth and boil it for an hour. Cut generous slices of pudding and place the slices in the pan beneath roasting meat, turning once. The slices will absorb the fat and juices and are a delicious accompaniment to a roast dinner. It is the Sussex equivalent of Yorkshire Pudding

Herb Pudding

Mix a tablespoon each of chopped parsley, thyme, dandelion and nettle leaves, onion, marjoram, basil, fennel, two handfuls of flour, one handful of chopped suet and a beaten egg. Put this mixture in a greased basin and boil or steam for two hours. Cut into slices and serve with meat dishes.

Arthur Blunden's Lark Pudding

This was made annually by Arthur Blunden, a landlord of the King's Head at East Hoathly in the reign of Queen Victoria, for Colonel Mardon, and cooked as a shooting lunch for six.

Half a pound each of steak and kidney, six larks, twelve oysters, quarter pound mushrooms, one small chopped shallot, pepper and salt, one tablespoon Lee & Perrin's Worcestershire Sauce, a grating of nutmeg, stock. Place the entire ingredients in a pudding bowl, cover with a substantial suet crust and boil for ten hours.

Savoury Meat Dumplings

Half a pound of flour, quarter of a pound of suet, quarter of a pound of cold meat diced, one teaspoon mixed herbs, one egg, pepper and salt. Mix the dry ingredients, add the beaten egg and sufficient water to get the right consistency. Roll into dumplings and boil for fifteen minutes. Serve with gravy.

Baked Fish Dumplings

Take equal quantities of cold boiled fish and cold mashed potatoes. Flake the fish and mix with the potato and sufficient anchovy past to moisten, roll out some puff past a quarter of an inch thick, cut into rounds, moisten the edges and put two tablespoonfuls of the fish mixture in each round, form into a dumpling, brush with egg and bake in a moderate oven for twenty minutes.

Rump Steak and Kidney Pudding

In one of her cookery books, Mrs Beeton wrote: 'The following recipe was contributed by a Sussex lady, in which county the inhabitants are noted for their savoury puddings'.

Two pounds rump steak, two kidneys, salt and pepper, suet crust made with milk in the proportion of six ounces to each one pound of flour. Procure some tender rump steak (that has been hung a little time). Line the dish with crust made of suet and flour, leaving a small piece of crust to overlap the edge. Then cover the bottom with a portion of the steak and a few pieces of kidney (some add a little flour to thicken the gravy, but this is not necessary), and then add another layer of steak, kidney and seasoning. Proceed in this manner till the dish is full, when pour in sufficient water to come within two inches of the top of the basin. Moisten the edges of the crust, cover the pudding over, press the two crusts together that the gravy may not escape, and turn up the overhanging paste. Wring out a cloth in hot water, flour it and tie up the pudding; put it into boiling water and let it boil at least four hours.

Poacher's Pudding

Mix together one pound of flour, half a pound of suet, one pound of boned, chopped rabbit, a large onion or leek, chopped, sage and thyme, pepper and salt. Boil it in a floured cloth, or a pudding basin for two to three hours.

This is a recipe from the Chichester area. Traditionally the pudding was served with greens and carrots. Sometimes pheasant was used instead of rabbit, in which case the feathers were always burnt on the fire so that nosy neighbours could not inform the gamekeeper that a little poaching had taken place.

Duck crusher

28

SWEET PUDDINGS

Sussex Pond Pudding

The custom was for Sussex Pond Pudding to be eaten on Palm Sunday and in some parts of the county it was known as Sussex Easter Pudding. Various versions have evolved over the years.

For the classic version the ingredients are eight ounces suet crust pasty, four ounces demerara sugar, four ounces flaked butter, one large lemon washed and pricked all over. Roll out the pastry into a large circle and use it to line a greased pudding basin. Pack in half the butter and sugar, place the lemon in the centre and cover with the rest of the butter and sugar. Make a lid from the trimmings and press it into place. Cover the pudding with buttered paper and a pudding cloth and steam it for three and a half hours. Serve with lemon sauce. Each person is given a piece of the lemon.

For another, usually more popular version, take the same amount of suet pastry, half a pound of butter, four ounces of sugar and a handful of raisins or currants. Make as before, using the dried fruit in place of the lemon. Alternatively work the fruit into the dough and have just the butter and sugar in the hollow – the pond.

A third version: Take half a pound of flour, half a pound of finely chopped suet, pinch of nutmeg, pinch of salt and tablespoon of sugar. Mix together with sufficient water to make a stiff paste. Divide into two equal portions. Roll out one to the thickness of your hand and in the centre place a quarter of a pound of butter and two tablespoons of sugar. Roll out the remaining portion of paste to the size and thickness of the first and lay it on top of the piece already prepared. Pinch the edges together place the pudding in a cloth and boil for four hours.

White Friars Pudding

Boil a good sized carrot until tender, rub it through a sieve. Chop a small apple finely, chop half a pound of suet. Wash and rub dry a quarter of a pound of currants, and a quarter of a pound of stoned raisins. Mix these together and add two tablespoons of treacle and half a salt spoon of mixed spice and by degrees, half a pound of flour. Add a little cold water if necessary. Beat to a stiff dough and place in a basin rubbed with dripping. Tie a cloth over and put the basin in a pan of boiling water. Boil for two hours.

Sussex recipe c 1830

29

Apple and Currant Dumplings

Half a pound of flour, quarter of a pound of suet, two ounces of sugar, one large apple diced, two ounces of currants, pinch of salt, water or sour milk. Mix the dry ingredients, add sour milk or cold water, roll into dumplings, boil for fifteen minutes, dust with powdered sugar and serve with golden syrup.

Jam Dumplings

Half a pound of flour, three ounces of suet, a pinch of salt, raspberry jam. Mix the dry ingredients into a smooth paste with a little water, roll out one inch thick, cut into rounds, moisten the edges, put a dessertspoonful of jam in the centre of each round, roll into dumplings and boil for fifteen minutes.

Swimmers

These were made with left over suet dough and were popular with children.

Drop little rolls of dough into boiling water and cook for about ten minutes. Drain and serve with a generous knob of butter and a sprinkling of brown sugar, or a spoonful of golden syrup. Swimmers were sometimes cooked in boiling stock and served with gravy before the main meal to fill up small stomachs.

Eve's Pudding

If you would have a good Pudding, pray mind what you're taught,
Take two penn'orth of eggs, when they're twelve for a groat.
And of the same juice which Eve once did taste,
When pared, and well chopped, half a dozen at least.
Six ounces of bread, let your maid eat the crust,
The crumbs must be grated as fine as fine dust.
Six ounces of currants, and pray pick them clean,
Lest they grate in your teeth, you know what I mean.
Six ounces of sugar won't make it too sweet,
With salt and some nutmeg to make it complete.
To this you may add, if you're willing and handy,
Some good lemon peel, and a large glass of brandy.
Three hours let it boil without hurry or flutter,
And then serve it up with some good melted butter.
Adam tasted and thought it was wondrous nice,
So Eve cut her husband another large slice.

Mrs Gould

Acres Pudding

Mix together six ounces suet, six ounces cleaned raisins, six ounces flour and a quarter pint of milk. Bake the pudding for about an hour in a square tin.

Sussex recipe c 1813

Marrowbone Pudding

Make a soft dough with one pound of flour, six ounces of suet, six ounces of sugar, a pinch of salt and a teaspoon of baking powder. Roll it into a square, place the marrow from a perfectly fresh marrowbone in the centre and fold the dough over it envelope fashion. Wrap it in a cloth and boil for three hours.

Sussex Blanket Pudding
(sweet or savoury)

Spread rolled out suet pastry with jam or syrup, roll up, pinch the edges together, tie in a floured cloth and boil for three hours. For the savoury version, spread the pastry with pieces of ham or bacon, slivers of liver, chopped onions and herbs.

SAVOURY PIES

Sussex Mock Pork Pie

Line a shallow pie dish with short or rough puff pastry. Arrange pieces of bacon (two to three ounces per person) in it, dust over with a pinch or more of mixed herbs, break one egg for each person into the pie, add pepper and salt to taste, cover with pastry and bake until golden. May be eaten hot or cold.

Sussex Shepherds' Pie

Cover the bottom of a casserole with one large chopped onion and four tablespoons of lentils. Season one tablespoon of flour with pepper, salt and half a teaspoon of curry powder and use this to coat four lamb chump chops. Place the chops on the lentils and pack one pound of small whole peeled potatoes around and on top. Sprinkle on any remaining flour and a tablespoon of brown sugar, add one pint of stock and cover. Cook on the middle shelf of the oven, on a low to medium heat, for three hours. Remove the lid for the last twenty minutes to brown.

Potato Pudding Pie

Boil two pounds of potatoes till soft, beat them in a mortar, and rub them through a sieve till quite fine. Mix in half a pound of fresh butter melted, beat up the yolks of eight eggs, and the whites of three. Add half a pound of white sugar pounded, half a pint of white wine, and stir them well together. Grate in half a nutmeg, and stir in half a pint of cream. Lay a good puff paste at the bottom, and round the edges of your dish, pour in your mixture, and bake it of a nice brown.

Susannah Stacey

SWEET PIES

An apple pie without the cheese
Is like a kiss without the squeeze
Sussex rhyme

Sussex Apple Pie

Edge a large pie dish with puff pastry. Place in the dish a sufficient quantity of peeled, cored and quartered apples until it is half full. Add sugar, a few cloves and the juice of half a lemon. Then add more apples, sugar, cloves and lemon juice until the dish is full. Boil the apple peelings, cores and a blade of mace in water and sugar to make a well flavoured syrup. Strain this over the apples and cover with a crust of puff pastry. While the pie is baking, beat the yolks of two new laid eggs with half a pint of cream, and sugar to sweeten. Cook this slowly, stirring all the time, until it almost boils. When the pie comes out of the oven cut a circle out of the crust and pour in the cream custard.

Apple and Cranberry Pie

Peel, core, quarter and re-quarter four or five large apples. Put a layer in the bottom of a pie dish, sprinkle with sugar and a few cranberries. Add a squeeze of lemon juice and thin lemon rind, about four cloves, several grates of nutmeg and sugar in moderation. Boil the cores and peelings of the apples in sugar and water for about half an hour and pour sufficient of this, strained, into the dish from time to time between layers of apple and cranberries until the dish is full, piling it up in the centre. Cover with a short crust made with butter and lard and good plain flour. Bake the pie for about three quarters of an hour in a moderate oven and serve with cream or with custard made from fresh eggs.

Edward Shoosmith

THE MEAT COURSE

Southdown sheep are today so uncommon in their native county that when exhibited at agricultural shows they are designated as a rare breed. The speckle faced Southdown is a small animal, well proportioned with a chunky body supported squarely on short, straight legs. It has a broad, level back and famously meaty rump and thigh.

Champion Southdown ewe

To Glynde farmer, John Ellmann, must go the credit for developing the stunted sheep that had cropped the Downs from time immemorial into a breed famous for both its meat and its wool. His advice was sought by agricultural deputations from abroad and by the land owners and noblemen of the eighteenth century. Excusing his late arrival at the Royal Pavilion in Brighton to the Prince Regent, the Duke of Bedford once said: 'Please, Your Royal Highness, I have been farming with my friend Ellman'.

Southdown sheep were exported around the world and the great breeding flocks of New Zealand and Australia were established by this breed. Ellman sold his flock for £3,910.16s in 1829 and left Glynde to live in retirement alternately at High Cross, Uckfield, and in Albion Street, Lewes. He died in 1832.

The success of the Southdown breed is also said to be due, in part, to their diet of the thyme-rich, close grown herbage of Downland and to the immense numbers of a small black spiralled white snails that they ate. It is an affable breed, developed through the Sussex practice of running the sheep on quite small areas, with the result that the flocks were familiar with their shepherds and accustomed to regular handling.

And on the subject of lamb – there is a grave in the cemetery at Broadwater, Worthing, said to contain the remains of Mary of 'little lamb' fame. Mary Hughes, neé Thomas, was born at Llangollen in 1841 and lived for many years in Worthing, where she died, aged ninety, in 1931. However, Mrs Hughes's claim to be the original Mary, who took her lamb to school one day, is disputed by those who claim that the poem entitled *Mary's Little Lamb* was written by an American, Sarah Josepha Hale, eleven years before Mary Hughes was born.

A pedigree Sussex cow

John Ellman also bred Sussex cattle – indeed he was so successful that he had to withdraw from competition at the shows around the county to give others a chance of winning a trophy.

The Sussex, a beast of ancient lineage, is an early maturing beef animal, hardy, able to flourish where other breeds would starve. Originally it was a draught animal, bred for work first and beef afterwards. Sussex oxen had to take their share of the work on the farm, pulling the plough, dragging the great farm waggons, the rollers and the harrows.

In fact the animals were not fattened until they were many years older than other breeds. At the fairs and markets there would be 'furriners from the sheers' – farmers from neighouring counties – competing to snap up the eleven or twelve year old beasts of burden to fatten and make a handsome profit. Age appeared to make no difference to the succulence of the beef.

'The cattle in this county are universally allowed to be equal to any in the Kingdom; the true cows are a deep red colour, the hair is fine and the skin is mellow, thin, and soft,' wrote Arthur Young in *The Annals* in 1795.

'The cow usually gives from one to two gallons of milk at a meal and from 3 to 4lbs of butter in the summer per week, the butter and milk are no objects where the system of raising their young stock is so well understood and so much more profitable.'

No part of a mutton or beef carcase was wasted. Hooves, ears, heads, tails, tongues, internal organs, bones – all had their uses. Verral concocted a dish of lambs' heads (cut out the eyes and chop off the nostrils) with parsley sauce; brains were broiled and served on rice; eyes were breadcrumbed and fried; tongues served au gratin. Docked lambs' tails were considered a great delicacy and were the the shepherds' perquisites, eaten with dumplings.

Jigot of Mutton with Spanish Onions

A jigot of mutton is the leg with part of the loin; provide such a one as has been killed two or three days at least, thump it well, and bind it with pack thread, that you keep whole when you take it out; put it into a pot about its bigness, and pour in a little of your broth (see page 12), and cover it with water; put in about a dozen Spanish onions, with the rinds on, three or four carrots, a turnip or two, some parsley, and any other herbs you like; cover down close, and stew it gently for three or four hours, but take your onions out after an hour's stewing, and take the first and second rinds off, put 'em into a stewpan with a ladle or two of your cullis (see page 13) a mushroom or two, or truffles minced, and a little parsley; take your mutton and drain it clean from the fat and liquor; make your sauce hot, and well seasoned, squeeze in a lemon, and serve it up with the onions round it, and pour the sauce over it.

William Verral

Lambs Ears with Sorrel

About a dozen of lambs ears will make a small dish, and they must be stewed tender in a braise; take a large handful of sorrel, chop it a little, and stew it in a spoonful of broth and a morsel of butter, pour in a small ladle of cullis (see page 13), a little pepper and salt, and nutmeg, stew it a few minutes, and dish up the ears upon it, nicely twisted up.

William Verral

Mutton and Marigold Broth

Take a scrag of mutton about six pounds and cut it in two. Boil half in a gallon of water and skim it well, adding a bundle of sweet herbs (marjoram, thyme, fennel, sage, parsley, a bay leaf and winter savory) an onion, a stick of celery and a good crust of bread. Let it boil one hour then put in the other part of the mutton. Take a turnip, a few chives chopped fine and a good plenty of dried marigold flowers and a little more parsley chopped fine. Put these in about a quarter of an hour before your broth is enough. Season suitably with salt.

Sussex, c 1760

Lambs' Heads

This used to be a favourite country dish in Downland towns and villages. Two heads and the scrag ends of the necks are carefully cleaned and blanched. In the stewpan with them are placed some good stock, half a lemon pared and sliced, a bunch of herbs, an onion, carrot and turnip. This is covered with some slices of fat bacon and stewed gently for three or four hours. The gravy is strained and seasoned; to this is added the yolks of three eggs well beaten and a tablespoonful of chopped parsley, and stirred over the fire until it thickens.

Mutton Hotpot

Cut two pounds of mutton or lamb into convenient pieces and roll them in seasoned flour. Brown in hot lard. Lay the meat in a casserole dish and cover with four sliced apples and two finely minced onions. Put on the lid and bake for two and a half hours in a moderate oven. Spread with red currant jelly before serving.

Surloin of Beef, The Fillet Hash'd

Trim your beef to look decent, and put it into a marinade the day before (two quarts of new milk, some green onions, a shallot or two, parsley, a little spice, whole pepper, salt, two or three bay leaves and some coriander seed). Wrap it up in paper to roast it; take out the inside fillet and slice it very thin; take care of your gravy, and put your meat into a stewpan with it, and as much of your cullis (see page 13) as is necessary to well fill the part where the meat was taken out, with some flowing in the dish; season with only pepper, salt, a shallot or two, and minced parsley; make it thorough boiling hot; add the juice of a lemon, and serve it up what we call the wrong side uppermost.

William Verral

Loaf of Beef-Collops

Order a loaf of French bread the size of your dish roll'd flattish, take out the inside, and fry the crust in butter; take as much of the fillet of a surloin, or the tender part of a rump of beef as will do for your loaf, hash it raw very thin, oil a bit of butter, and fry it quick, season with only a morsel of onion and parsley minced; for the sauce take a large ladle or two of cullis, season with pepper, salt and nutmeg, a mushroom or two and shallots minced very fine; stew this a few minutes, and put in the hash; but do not let it boil a minute after; squeeze the juice of a lemon or orange, pour it in and over your loaf and serve it up.   *William Verral*

To Fry Beef Steaks

Take ye steeks and fry them gently without any butter, then put them to ye hind part of ye pan, and put to ye gravy, half a pint of water, a little sweet margeram, a little thyme, & a little onion shred small, & let it boil a little together, then put in a peas of butter, & flower ye steeks & stew them a little over ye fire, grat in some nutmeg   *Philadelphia Shoebridge*

To Hash a Calfes Head

Take a Calfe head & Cleanse it & take out ye braines & three parts boyle ye head, & when it is so boyled take it out & lett it coole. Then cut ye meat from ye bones in little thin slices & put it in a stew pan & season it with cloves, mace, nuttmegg, peper & salt & put to it a glasse of Clarrett wine & sweet butter & bunch of sweet hearbs & lett it stew, boyle ye braines & when they are boyld beate them with ye yolks of two or three raw eggs & a little sack & put in a sprigg of time & mince it small & season it with Cloves, mace, nuttmegg, pepper & salt & put in a little flower. Mix it well together then take a frying pan & heate it hott with a peace of fresh butter & put it in by spoonfulls & fry them like friters. When they are browne take them out & sett them before the fire, this being done take a couple of Anchoveys & two or three cloves of Sharlott, mince them small together & put it in to ye hash & shake it together & put in a bay lefe and a few capers & some pickled oysters & mushrooms & shake it together & when you think that ye hash is (cooked) enough take ye yoke of an egge & beat it with a little wine & put it in & shake it together; have a Care it doe not curdle, & wring in ye juice of a Lemon in it. Broile the jawbones & put them in the dish, then power on the hash & garnish ye dish with Lemon & Oranges & the fryed brains & some thin slices of bacon fryed & laid about.
Arundel ms

Chiddingly Hot Pot

Take a large earthenware casserole, and place in the bottom some chopped or sliced onions or shallots, and celery, with chopped olives and olive vinegar. Then put in a layer of sirloin beef and sprinkle with allspice, cloves and black pepper, add a piece or two of unground mace and some olive vinegar. Cover with thinly sliced raw potatoes and more chopped olives. Add another layer of beef on top of which place a layer of chopped olives and finish off with onions and celery then more sliced potatoes. Add water to all but cover and place the casserole in an oven overnight after the fire has gone down (or set the oven at its lowest setting). Heat the casserole in a hot oven about half an hour before it is required the next day.
Edward Shoosmith, 1917

Beef a la Mode

Take a small buttock of beef, tie with string. Take mace, pepper and salt to taste, and pound lards of bacon with this seasoning and lard ye beef with it very thick. Have in readiness a stewpan with boiling hot butter. Put beef in, first one end and then ye other till they are very brown. Put it in a pot with as much good broth as will cover it and stew in all sorts of spices and sweetherbs with 2/3 large onions, a turnip or two and carrot cut in pieces. Stew for 4/6 hours, check that it is tender. Make the sauce of some of the liquor with 2/3 anchovies and mushrooms thickened up with a little brown butter and claret. Serve with forc'd meat balls if liked.
Thomas Frewen

To Make a Beef Tansey

Take seven eggs, putting out two Whites; put to them a full Pint of Cream, a little Nutmeg, & a few sweet Herbs, as Thime, sweet Marjerom, Parsly, Strawberry leaves, shred them very small; then take boiled Beef mincd very small a full plate of White bread grated, mixe them all together, & fry them as you doe other Tansies, but not too brown.
Philadelphia Shoebridge

To Dress ye Veal ye French way called Blanket

Take part of a fillet of veal after it is roasted. Cut it into very thin and small slices then beat ye yolks of 4 eggs and put to 'em about a pint of cream and a good quantity of parsley cut very small. Then take about half pound of butter and when boiled in your stewpan put in ye veal, let it fry a little while, then put to it ye mixture of cream etc, a little chives if ye like 'em,

38

chopt very small, then serve it up with slices of lemon. If the sauce is too thick thin it with milk before you turn it out of the stewpan. When veal is put in the pan shake over it a little grated nutmeg or pounded mace and some sack.

Thomas Frewen

Sussex Rabbit Casserole

Joint one large or two small rabbits and soak overnight in cold water. Dry and roll in seasoned flour. Cut half a pound of unsmoked streaky bacon into strips; blanch and drain. Put the rabbit, bacon, pepper and salt and two tablespoons of finely chopped fresh sage in a deep ovenproof dish. Pour on two fluid ounces of milk. Cook one pound of sliced onions in two ounces of butter until the onions begin to turn brown. Cool the onions then add half a pound of fresh breadcrumbs, the grated rind of a lemon and a handful of chopped parsley, mix and add an egg and a little milk to bind. Spread the onion mixture on top of the rabbit and cook in a slow to moderate oven for two hours.

Rabbit Stew

Joint two young rabbits, dredge the joints with flour and fry in butter to a light brown. Add half a pint of good stock, half a pint of ale or stout, half a cup of mushroom ketchup, a little grated nutmeg and lemon peel and an onion stuck with cloves, and stew for an hour.

Jugged Hare

Simmer the hare for four or five hours with some good beef steak in the pot, a glass of red wine added to the gravy just before serving and plenty of redcurrant jelly and forcemeat balls and mashed turnips.

Rabbit Rissoles

Mince rabbit meat finely with fat bacon and a pinch of mixed herbs, add mashed potato, form into flat round cakes, roll in egg and breadcrumbs and fry.

SEA AND FRESHWATER FISH

Watch, barrel, watch!
Mackerel for to catch,
White may they be like blossom on a tree.
Some by their heads and some by their tails.
God sends thousands and never fails.
Old Fisherman's Chant

Oysters once bred so prolifically at every inlet along the Sussex coast that they were among the cheapest and most available of foods. Archaeological digs on Roman sites around Chichester often unearth mountainous piles of oyster shells, evidence of the teeming beds in the harbour.

The decline of the native oyster was attributed to a parasite brought in on the keels of ships. The smaller, thinner shelled native bivalves were less well adapted to withstand the attack than the thicker shelled foreign oysters.

In the past there was an abundance of both sea and river fish. Each year great mackerel shoals arrived offshore in the last week of April or the first of May – although Sussex people would not eat mackerel until the elm trees were in leaf.

Before the boats set off for the first catch a custom called Bending-in had to be observed. This took place on the beach and included a feast of bread, cheese and beer provided by the boat owners for the fishermen, their wives and children. The nets were folded on the beach and blessed by a priest. The term 'bending-in' comes either from the priest's benediction, or from the gathering in of the folded (bent) nets to the boats. The practice died out around the turn of the century when the mackeral shoals moved away.

The herring catch was equally generous. On October 13,1788 a Brighton boat put to sea in the afternoon and returned before midnight with 33,500 herring – so many that her gunwale was barely above the surface of the water.

Around the chalk boulders at the foot of the cliffs there are winkles and dog whelks, limpets and piddocks to have for the taking at low tide. There was uproar in the 1950s when the Sussex coast suffered an annual invasion by the French. They, having scraped their own rocks bare long before, arrived in great numbers on the overnight Dieppe-Newhaven ferry to fill their sacks with ingredients for the famous Normandy fruits de mer dishes, returning home on the late boat.

Inland towns and villages had their fish delivered by dog cart – or, as at Lewes, by juggs. These were wide, flat baskets carried over the Downs from Brighton, along Juggs Road, by fishwives. Around the time when Victoria was newly on her throne there was a regular dog drawn cart running a circular route from Brighton through Lewes, Upper Dicker, Alfriston, Seaford, Newhaven and back to Brighton. Another went north to Ditchling, Hassocks, Burgess Hill, Hurstpierpoint and Cuckfield. Depending on the load there were two, four or six dogs to a team.

Herrings rot quickly, but villagers had a means of dealing with them. The fish were threaded on a pole which was hung in the chimney corner. When dried they were pulled off and clapped on to the gridiron as required.

Scallops, now a delicacy, were then a favourite food of the poor. Boats *Double hanging gridiron* brought them up river to Lewes, tying up at the steps below Cliffe Bridge where scallops were sold for twopence a dozen.

A small scallop called a queenie was sold from barrows in the streets of the coastal towns, and sometimes chinkerberries were available. These were scallops from a particular spot in the Channel from where a bearing could be taken on Chanctonbury Ring. The scallops were usually poached in water for a few minutes, dusted with flour and then fried.

As for freshwater fish – the rivers teemed with roach, bream and perch, with salmon, mullet, trout and carp. Long ago the Ouse was famous for its salmon. Thousands returned each year to spawn but the small mesh nets used to catch them wiped out the entire stock.

Leonard Mascall, who lived at Plumpton Place, was the author of a number of books on animal husbandry and was credited by some of his contemporaries with introducing the carp to England in the reign of Henry VIII. But carp had existed in monastic stews since at least the early 1400s. As the old rhyme records:

Turkeys, Carp, Hops, Pickerell and Beer,
Which came into England all in one yeare.

Carp is a muddy flavoured fish and the monks cooked it in wine – otherwise 'clean pebbles, cleaner water, cleansing salt, many washings and purifications many times repeated' was the recommended preparation for the fish.

Eels, like many other foods, were used as a form of currency. Where the tenants of Bosham Manor, for instance, paid rent at the rate of 700 oysters yearly, those living in Northease and Southease had to supply 2,000 eels a year as their dues.

Mackerel Pudding

Put a cloth in a pudding basin, line it with good suet crust, fill it with boned mackerel, pepper and salt and a few bay leaves. Diced belly of pork may also be added if desired. Put on a lid of suet crust and pinch the edges well together. Tie the cloth tightly and boil for about three hours.

Brighton fisherfolk recipe

Brighton Mackerel

Clean the fish and cut off their heads. Dry them and roll them in flour and fry on both sides in butter. Serve with fried onions and mustard sauce (made with half ounce butter, half ounce flour, large teaspoon mustard powder, pinch of sugar, an ounce of grated cheese and sufficient milk/water to give the correct consistency).

Soused Mackerel

Clean the mackerel and cut off the heads. Dry them and lay them in a saucepan. Sprinkle with salt, pepper, a pinch of pickling spices, a little made mustard, a pinch or two of sugar, a bayleaf and just enough vinegar and water (two parts vinegar to one of water) to cover. Bring to the boil, lower the heat and simmer for 15–20 minutes.

William Verral

Fillets of Soles with Herbs in a Brown Sauce

Skin your soles both sides, and lay them a while in a marinade of white wine, &c., dry them well in a cloth and fry them without butter or flour, of a nice colour; take off your fillets nicely, cut them into pieces in length about two inches, put them into a stewpan with a glass of Champagne or Rhenish, pepper, salt and nutmeg, a small ladle of gravy or cullis mixt; mince separate, a green truffle or mushroom, a leaf or two of pimpernell, a little sweet basil, thyme and parsley, and a morsel of shallot; put into your gravy, &c. such a quantity of each as you like best; stew all together very gently for a quarter of an hour, squeeze in the juice of a lemon or orange, and serve it up very hot.

William Verral

Lobster Pye

Crack two medium sized lobsters; take out the meat as whole as you can; season it with pepper, salt and mace. Then mix the cream and berries (contents of head and coral) with half a pint of scalded cream; let the berries be well bruised and mixed. Lay a thin paste round your dish; lay in your seasoned lobster. Divide up then half a pound of butter in three parts and put one bit at the bottom, one in the middle and one at the top, with hard yolks of eggs and a few oysters and their liquor. Put on a cover of paste and bake it in an oven. Have ready warmed your cream and berries, lift the cover and pour it over the pye and replace the cover.

MS cookery book of 1795

Eel pudding

Take two medium size eels, the third of their weight of pickled pork, a little chopped parsley and shallot, two hard boiled eggs, pepper, salt and suet crust. Skin, clean and bone the eels, cut them and the pork into convenient pieces; chop the shallots and pass them in butter for a few minutes. Line a pudding basin with suet crust, put in the eels, shallots, pork, chopped eggs and chopped parsley, pepper and salt. Fill up with a stock made with the heads, tails and other trimmings of the eels, cover with suet crust and boil for two and a half hours. *Miss Gould*

To Stew Eels

Trim, cut and fry the eels, which may be done the evening before, take three anchovies, three bay leaves, a small onion, some whole pepper and allspice, some horse-radish, two spoonsfuls of port wine and one of vinegar, some lemon peel and a little water. Put in the eels and stew all together for twenty minutes.

Collared eel

Catch your eel, cut off the fins, split it or take out the bones, lay it flat on its back, grate over it some nutmeg, two or three blades of mace, a handful of parsley, shredded fine, with a few sage leaves, pepper and salt. Roll it up, tie it in a cloth, and boil it in salt and water for three quarters of an hour. May be eaten hot or cold.

Sarah Gillow 1807-1866

To Stew Oysters

Take yr great oysters & a Little of ye Liquor, a pint of white wine, two anchovys, a little nutmeg sliced, two or three blades of whole mace, a bunch of sweet herbs. Let it stew near a quarter of an hour, then put in a quarter of a pound of sweet butter. Serve it with sipetts, Barberys & Lemon.

Arundel ms

Sussex Smokie

Take one pound of filleted, skinned, smoked haddock, two ounces of butter, two ounces of flour, half a pint of milk, four ounces of cheddar cheese, one glass of dry white wine, black pepper, a bay leaf and grated Parmesan cheese. Poach the haddock in one and a half pints of water with the bay leaf. Cool slightly. Grate the cheddar cheese, melt the butter in a saucepan and add the flour to form a roux. After two or three minutes slowly pour in half a pint of the stock from the poached haddock and the milk, stirring all the time. Bring to the boil and simmer for a few minutes, stirring all the time. Add the grated cheese, black pepper and wine and continue to cook until smooth. Finally add flaked haddock and spoon the mixture into six small ramekins. Sprinkle the Parmesan on top. If serving immediately, heat the ramekins under a grill until the Parmesan goes golden-brown. Otherwise put the ramekins in a hot oven for ten minutes before serving.

Marion Briggs, Ringmer

Cockle Soup

Boil your cockles and take them out of the shells, then wash them and put them into a saucepan. Take 2 or 3 lbs of fresh fish and a cullis as for crayfish soup, strain it through a sieve to the thickness of a cream and put to it a little of your cockles. Cut off the top of a French roll and take out the crumbs and fry it in a little butter; place it in the middle of your soup dish, the bread being soaked with a little of your cullis. Garnish with a rim of paste, lay the cockle shells round the outside, thicken up the cockles with a yolk of egg as you would for a Fricassee, and put one or two in each shell round the soup, also fill up the loaf in the middle. The cullis being boiling hot, squeeze into it and on to the cockles a little lemon and serve it up.

Arundel Mullet

Grey mullet

The mullet must be boiled in salt and water. When done, remove the mullet, pour away part of the water and put in a pint of red wine, some salt and vinegar, two onions sliced with a bunch of sweet herbs, some nutmeg, beaten mace and the juice of a lemon. Boil these well with two or three anchovies, put in the fish and when simmered some time, put them into a dish and strain the sauce over them. Shrimp or oyster may be added.

Mary Bays

Fried Mullets

Scale and gut the fish, score them across the back and dip them in melted butter. Clarify some butter, fry the mullets in it, and when done lay them on a warm dish, and serve them with anchovy and butter for sauce.

Mary Bays

45

To Bake Mullets

Scale, draw, wash and dry your Mullets, then lard them with salted eel, season them and make a Pudding (stuffing) for them with grated bread, fresh eel minced, sweet herbs, salt nutmeg, the yolks of hard eggs and anchovies, minced small. Put this in the bellies of your Mullets if you keep them whole. If not, cut them in four pieces, season them with pepper, ginger or nutmeg and lay them in your Pye. Make balls of your farce and lay them upon the pieces of Mullet, then lay on also prawns or cockles, yolks of eggs minced, large mace, Butter and Barberries and close up your Pye. When it is baked, close up the lid and stick it full of lozenges, cuts of paste and other garnishes. Fill it up with beaten butter and garnish it with slices of Lemons.

Cookery book of John Nott (1726) cook to Lord Ashburnham

Potted Shrimps

Boil the shrimps in strong salt and water until done, then shell them. Put them into small pots with plenty of fresh ground black pepper and a little mace, press well down then fill up the pots with clarified butter.

M K Samuelson

WILD AND DOMESTIC FOWL

WILD birds were eaten by the thousands in the Sussex country-side in less preservation conscious days. Many villages had a Sparrow and Rat Club, the members of which saved the heads of all the sparrows, finches, blackbirds, magpies, larks, thrushes, rooks and other birds and tails of rats caught, and competed annually for prizes for the highest numbers. Any member not producing 100 heads and tails by March 1 was fined sixpence.

Up to the early years of this century, Sussex shepherds supple-mented their pay by trapping wheatears on the Downs. These little birds, about six inches long, with black beak, legs and claws, arrived in March, en route from Africa to Scotland and Scandinavia. A few would nest in Sussex, in a heap of stones, crevices in chalk pits or seaside cliffs, in deserted rabbit burrows – but most continued north. On their return south they rested on the Downs for a period of around six week – which was when open season was declared on the wheatear, birds that arrived when the wheat was ripe.

Shepherds prepared coops to trap them and visited each coop twice a day to harvest the catch. The greatest number were taken near Beachy Head; on occasions up to fifty or eighty dozens.

The wheaters, birds that were considered to be a great delicacy, almost the equal of the ortolan, were sold to poulterers for a penny each. If Downland walkers took birds from the coops it was the cus-tom to leave a penny for each bird taken.

Because the small birds were so naturally larded with lumps of fat they perished quickly and no conveyance was swift enough to take

Wheatear trap

them to London before they had putrified. Not, that is, until the arrival of the train.

Wheatears are said to have saved the life of William Wilson, lord of the manor of Eastbourne, in 1658. In Commonwealth England Wilson remained loyal to the Stuarts and on Good Friday of that year Cromwell sent a detachment of dragoons commanded by Lieutenant Hopkins to Compton Place to search for incriminating documents.

When the Roundheads arrived, Wilson was ill in bed and his wife served up to them a large wheatear pie. A contemporary account reports: 'The officer, it being quite a novelty to him, was equally amazed and delighted, and merrily insisted that all his military companions should taste of the rare repast, which they did with much jollity'.

Meanwhile, Mrs Wilson hurried upstairs and burned the incriminating papers so that when Lieutenant Hopkins, sated with wheatear pie, arrived to inspect the files, there was nothing to find. 'Had I found anything according to the information given in against him, my orders were to have taken him away,' the officer said. After the Restoration, Charles II created a baronetcy for the Wilsons and wheatears formed a conspicuous quartering in the coat of arms.

A popular method of cooking both wheatears and larks was to thread the small birds on a spit with pieces of fat bacon between, and to roast them over an open fire, basting with drippings or butter. Breadcrumbs were sprinkled over them and they were cooked some more until they browned.

Chicken fattening was a major industry in the Heathfield area. Kezia Collins of Keeper's Hut, Cade Street, is said to have started the business in 1788 by taking in lean fowls, crating them and cramming them by hand to produce plump, succulent birds in just four weeks. The crating, an early example of today's factory farmed chicken, was not new even then.

Two hundred years earlier, in his book, *The Husbandlye Ordring and Governmente of Poultrie*, Leonard Mascall said that birds for fattening should be kept in a warm, dark place, each penned separately 'so closely as to restrict its movement'.

Mrs Collins' business proved profitable and soon cottagers and farmers' wives in many of the neighbouring villages took to fattening poultry. Cramming machines were introduced around 1840. A tube was inserted into the bird's crop and the machine force fed it a mixture of milk, fat and ground oats.

The coming of the railway to Heathfield in 1880 boosted business considerably. Until then fowls fattened for the London market were carried by road, through the thick Wealden mud in winter and on the hard, heavily rutted roads in summer. In the year the station opened at Heathfield £60,000 worth of poultry was transported to the London markets, and by 1894 this had risen to £140,000.

Huffed Chicken

Stuff four skinned and boned chicken breasts with four ounces of stoned and chopped prunes, four ounces of peeled, cored and chopped cooking apple, one large chopped onion, an ounce of fresh breadcrumbs, the grated rind of half a lemon, pepper and salt and a small beaten egg. Wrap each breast in suet pastry, tie it in a pudding cloth and boil for several hours.

Farmhouse Chicken

Cut a good roasting fowl into joints and flour. Fry a large onion in butter in a baking tin, stir in a tablespoon of flour then add the chicken, some chopped parsley, a little thyme fresh from the garden, two rashers of bacon cut into strips, pepper and salt. Cover with water and put a thick layer of breadcrumbs over all. Add one or two dabs of butter on the top and bake in a slow oven for two hours.

Early nineteenth century recipe from West Sussex

Poultry in Strawberry Leaves

Gather strawberry leaves on Lamas Eve and press them firmly until the perfume becomes sensible. Take a fat bird, pluck him and enfold him in the pressed leaves. Put in a fire proof dish, add a little water, some rosemary, lavender flowers and other sweet smelling herbs, half a pound of butter and a pint of white wine. Cook in the oven and, when ready, remove the leaves, strain the juice and serve it with the bird, adding a little salt.

A Savory and Boyled Capon

Take a fatt fleshy Capon or hen, dress it in ye ordinary way & clense it within from ye gutts, then put in ye fatt again into ye belly & splitt ye bones of ye leggs & wings as far as you may not to deface ye fowle, so as ye marrow may stil out of them. Add a little marrow to it, season it with peper, salt & what other spice you like & savory herbs, dates, Currans, Raisons, & sugar. Putt all these with ye Capon in a Large ox bladder first well scowred with wine, and tye it very fast & close on ye top that nothing may come out or gett in, but let there be roome enough in ye bladder for ye flesh to swell & farment. Put this to boyle for two hours in a kettle of water or till by touching it you find ye capon tender, then serve it up in a dish in ye bladder. When you cut the bladder you will find a savory dish.

Arundel ms

To Roast a Turkey

You must make your forced meat with Pork as much fat as lean, & season it with ye same seasoning and herbs, spinage, sage, thyme, parsley, pepper, nutmeg, & put it into ye breast of your Turkey with lemon pill (peel), thyme & bacon & roast. Make your sauce with a little gravy, anchovy, a little pepper & a blade of mace, a little white wine if you have no gravy, & an onion, & season it with Salt. When it boyle that your anchovy is dissolved, melt in a good piece of butter, & put it into ye dish with your Turkey.

Philadelphia Shoebridge

To Stew Pidgions White

Take twelve Pidgions with their Giblets & Quarter them & put them in a stew pan with four Blades of mace, a little peper & salt some herbs & just water enough to stew them without Burning, add Onion. Let ye fire be clear but not fierce, when they are tender thicken ye Liquor with ye yolks of two eggs, six or seven spoonfuls of sweet cream, a little butter, & a little shread time & Parsley. Shake them all together, garnish with Lemon and what you please.

Arundel ms

Sheila Kaye-Smith in her book *Kitchen Fugue* (1945), described the rite for cooking the oldest inhabitant of the farmyard – her duck Waddleby, which had ceased to lay the eggs that ensured her existence in wartime England.

'Waddleby made a glorious end – that is my great comfort. I do not refer to her behaviour on the scaffold, of which I took care to have no knowledge, but of her almost apocalyptic passing into our systems in the form of roast duck.

'Yes, roast duck. For though Waddleby was three years old, and had a mileage of probably three figures, she "cut up" as tender, succulent and juicy as any duckling. This miracle was achieved by an old cook of mine, who came out from the seaside town to perform the ceremony. The recipe is applicable to elderly hens as well as elderly ducks.

'First hang the carcase for as long as you possibly can, according to the weather. On the evening before the ceremony take an egg cup full of whisky and with a pastry brush paint it over the entire skin. This is essential. The magic does not work without whisky. Repeat this two or three times on the day itself, presupposing that the meal is in the evening; if it is at midday, everything must be started earlier.

'Put the carcase in a covered roasting tin into which you have poured water instead of fat, and cook in a brisk oven until all the water has evaporated, which should take about an hour. The reason for the whisky is now apparent, for you are steaming your bird; the action of the alcohol on the skin will prevent this getting soggy, after the manner of those aged fowls which appeared as *poulet roti* in certain restaurants even before the war. When all the water is gone, lower the heat, put dripping into the tin and baste frequently till the bird is cooked, which should take another two hours.'

VEGETABLES AND HERBS

Dearly beloved brethren,
Is it not a sin,
When you peel potatoes
To throw away the skin?
For the skin feeds the pigs,
And the pigs feed you.
Dearly beloved brethren,
Isn't that true?

Samphire – sea spinach – used to be abundant on the chalk cliffs especially on the Seven Sisters headlands between Cuckmere Haven and Beachy Head. Known as the herb of St Peter, it was prized by gourmets who ate the young leaves raw in salads, cooked and ate it like asparagus and pickled it to serve with cold mutton.

Samphire was also used as a cleansing medicine and to help digestion, and it was considered an excellent remedy for rheumatism because of the salt and iodine content. It is a fleshy plant similar to an ice plant, or a mesembryanthemum, to which it is distantly related. Flowers are produced from June to September and the seeds contain an aromatic oil.

Hops were also once used as a salad ingredient. They were boiled in salt and water and dressed with oil, vinegar, pepper and salt. The young leaves of violet plants were another piquant ingredient of a green salad.

A vegetable that used to be common on Sussex tables is sherdoone, a wild thistle found in hedges and ditches. The usual method of cooking it was to cut the stalks into ten inch lengths, tie them in bundles and boil them like asparagus. Alternatively the stalks could be cut into dice, boiled like peas and tossed in pepper, salt and butter.

Cottage gardeners used to blanch growing dandelion plants by placing drain pipes over them until the leaves had turned white. A salad was then made with the white leaves, watercress and vinegar.

Marrow has always been a vegetable of many uses – jam, chutney, as a vegetable and for soup. A traditional Sussex dish is marrow pie, made with a hard, ripe marrow, cut up and boiled with sugar, ground ginger, currants, sultanas and peel, covered with short pastry and baked.

Fried Marrow

Peel very young marrows and cut them into rings. Dip rings in stiff batter and fry in deep fat. Parsnips can be fried the same way, but the vegetables have first to be boiled until soft before they are cut into rings.

Sorrel and Leek Pie

Line a pie plate with good short pastry and put in a layer of sorrel (plenty as it shrinks), a layer of bacon, a layer of leeks, sliced, more bacon and a final layer of sorrel plus pepper and salt. Cover with pastry and bake in a gentle oven for about an hour and a half.

Leek Pie

Sweat cleaned, sliced leeks in butter, place in a pie with five snipped rashers of streaky bacon, two beaten eggs and a quarter of a pint of cream, cover with short pasty and bake in a moderate oven until golden.

Old Claverham Potato Cakes

To six middling-size potatoes put one quart flour; boil the potatoes till they are very soft. Mash them with a piece of butter, the size of a walnut, till they are smooth; rub them into the flour very lightly with a little salt, lay them lightening with a little good yeast; when risen wet them with warm milk and mix into a stiff batter, beating them well; use flour enough to mould them, put them at a distance from the fire to keep warm, let them stand three hours, then roll them out, and put them on tins near the fire till they rise well; prick them with a fork, wash lightly with milk, and bake them in a slack oven 20 minutes.

A slack oven is a Sussex term to describe the heat of a brick oven after the bread had been baked and taken out.

Shoosmith family recipe

53

Ten To One Pie
(ten pieces of potato to one of meat)

Line a pie plate with pastry and fill with a layer of thinly sliced raw potatoes, a layer of sliced onion, a layer of pickled pork, pepper and salt, then
more layers of potatoes and onions. Cover with pastry and bake for an
hour and a half.

Spinach with Cream and Eggs

Scald spinach in a morsel of butter and water and salt, press the juice from
it very dry and chop it small and put it in a stew pan with about half a pint
of cream, a morsel of butter and flour, a whole old onion, pepper and salt
and a little nutmeg, take out your onion, squeeze in an orange or lemon
and dish it up. Garnish with hard eggs cut in two or bits of bread nicely
fry'd.
William Verral

Spinach Pudding

Pick and wash a quarter of a peck of spinach, put it into a saucepan, with a
little salt, cover close, and when boiled tender, throw it into a sieve to
drain. Chop it with a knife, beat up six eggs, and mix it with half a pint of
cream, a stale roll grated fine, nutmeg, and a quarter of a pound of melted
butter. Stir well together, put it into the saucepan in which you boiled the
spinach, and stir it till it thickens. Then wet and flour the cloth, tie it up,
and boil it an hour. When done, turn it into a dish, pour melted butter
over, with the juice of a Seville orange; strew on it a little grated sugar, and
serve it hot.
Susannah Stacey

Pease with Onion

Let your pease be very young, put them in a stew pan with a bit of bacon
with some cloves stuck in, pour in a ladle of broth (see page 12), a bunch of
onions and parsley, pepper and a little salt if it is required, stew them gently till almost dry, take out the bacon and herbs and put about a gill of
cream, a bit of butter and flour mixt, let it go gently on about ten minutes,
squeeze in the juice of lemon or orange and dish them up very hot.
William Verral

Onion Pie

Line a pie dish with short pastry and fill with layers of thinly sliced potatoes, left-over cooked meat and onions until the dish is full, finishing with
an onion layer, Season, add thickened stock, place a pastry lid on and cook
in a moderate oven until the pastry is golden.

Vegetable Pie

Scald and blanch broad beans; cut young carrots, turnips, artichoke bottoms, mushrooms, pease, onions, lettuce, parsley, celery, or any of them you have; make the whole into a nice stew. Bake a crust over a dish, a little lining round the edge, with a cup turned up to keep it from sinking. When baked, open the lid, and pour in the stew

Susannah Stacey

Artichoke Pie

Boil twelve artichokes, break off the leaves and chokes, and take the bottoms from the stalks. Make a good puff paste crust, and spread a quarter of a pound of fresh butter over the bottom of your pie. Then a row of artichokes, strew pepper, salt, and beaten mace over them, then another row, strew the rest of your spice, and put in a quarter of a pound more butter cut in bits. Boil half an ounce of truffles and morels, in a quarter of a pint of water. Pour the water into the pie, cut the truffles and morels very small and throw them all over the pie. Pour in a gill of white wine, cover, and bake it.

Susannah Stacey

Herb Pie

Pick two handfuls of parsley, half the quantity of spinach, two lettuces, mustard and cresses, a few leaves of burridge, and white beet leaves; wash, and boil them a little; drain, press out the water; cut them small; mix and lay them in a dish, sprinkled with salt. Mix a batter with flour, two eggs well beaten, a pint of cream, and half a pint of milk, and pour it on to the herbs. Cover with a good crust, and bake it.

Susannah Stacey

Colcanon

Boil some good greens and chop them as for bubble and squeak, then take an equal quantity of potatoes mashed, mixing the whole together in a mould with pepper, salt and butter. Serve it up hot.

Wiston House 1800

Cheesy Parsnips

Fill an oven dish with cooked parsnips cut into rough chunks and pour over them a strong cheese sauce. Top with grated cheese, breadcrumbs and knobs of butter and place in a hot oven until the top has browned.

TRUFFLES, MORELS AND MUSHROOMS

West Sussex used to be good truffle hunting territory, especially in the beech woods around Chichester, Slindon, Eartham and Goodwood. There was a lucrative trade in truffles in the early years of the nineteenth century when the best fetched ten to fifteen shillings a pound in London.

The hunters used trained dogs, usually poodles, or French barbets which, because they were not sporting dogs, were unlikely to be lured away from the job by the scent of game. The dogs were trained with a worsted ball kept in a truffle bag and buried. Earlier, truffle hunting pigs were used. The hogs, though, had a serious fault; unless the hunters were very quick, the porkers ate the truffles as soon as they found them.

Truffles are tubers ranging in size between that of a large plum and a large potato, found between two and seven inches beneath the ground and detected by their earthy smell. They ripen around the middle of August when the scent becomes very strong. They have vanished from the Sussex beech woods, and morels, another form of fungi once common in the county, have also disappeared.

Dressed truffles

First of all, lay them to soak some time in water, then brush them with a hard brush for they grow in stiff clayey ground, so that it is no easy matter to make them clean. Put them into as much claret or Burgundy as will cover them, a large onion or two, a bunch of herbs, whole pepper and some spices; let them simmer gently for about half an hour and send them to table hot in a napkin; pepper and salt is the general sauce for them. Preserve your wine they are boil'd in, it gives an excellent flavour to cullis or gravy.

William Verral

Truffle Pie

A pound of veal, quarter of a pound of lean ham, half a pound of ham fat, four ounces of bone marrow and six blanched livers chopped finely. Put these in a stew pan with chopped truffles, parsley, shallot, thyme, cayenne pepper and salt and cook for a few minutes, stirring, until the veal becomes white. When cool pound the mixture in a mortar and rub through a hair sieve. Use this to half fill the prepared pastry case, and lay a pound of braised, peeled truffles on top, with slices of fat ham to cover. Place the pastry lid on the pie and ornament it and cook it in a slow oven. When ready cut off the top and pour in a glass of Madeira wine.

Pickled mushrooms were said to be 'above truffles, above caviar and oysters' in flavour. After a mushroom picking expedition the large flat mushrooms were used for ketchup, the medium-sized mushrooms fried and eaten for breakfast, or dried for another day, and only the button mushrooms were used for pickling.

Pickled Mushrooms

Pour very hot salted water over the mushrooms, leave for a while then pour it away, replacing it with spiced vinegar just off the boil. Pack into glass jars and cork or seal immediately. Put aside for a few weeks before using.

Dried Mushrooms

Dry and peel the mushrooms and arrange them in rows on squares of blotting paper, then place them carefully on the racks in the oven, turning the temperature down to cool. When the mushrooms have dried completely, thread them on thick linen thread to use as required. Dropped into stews and casseroles the dried mushrooms regain their former plumpness.

Broiled Mushrooms

Stem and peel large open mushrooms. Put them on the gridiron, stem side down, over a bright but not very hot fire, and cook for three minutes. Turn them and put a small piece of butter in the middle of each, and broil for about ten minutes longer. Put them on hot plates, gills upward, and place another small piece of butter on each together with a little pepper and salt, and flavour with lemon juice, and place them in the oven for a minute or two.

To Stew Mushrooms

Take them fresh gathered, & cut off ye hard end of ye stalk, & as you pull them throw in a drop of white wine; after they have lyen half an hour drain them from ye wine, & put them between 2 silver dishes, & set them on a soft fire without any liquor, when they have so stewed a Little while, pour away ye liquor that comes from them, which will be very black. Then put ye mushroms into another dish with a sprig or two of thyme, a whole onion, four or five Corns of whole pepper, three or four cloves, a bit of an orange, a little salt, a bitt of sweet butter & some pure gravy of mutton. Cover them & set them on a gentle fire, & let them stew softly till they be enough & very tender. When you dish them blow off all ye fatt from them, & take out ye thyme & spice & orange. Then wring in ye juice of a Lemon & a little grated nutmeg, toss them two or three times & serve them hott.

Mushroom Loaves

Wash button mushrooms; boil them a few minutes in water, and put to them two spoonfuls of cream, butter rolled in flour, salt and pepper. Boil these up, then make a hole at the top of little round loaves, and fill your loaves with the mushrooms. Lay a bit of crust on the top of each, and put them in the oven to crisp.

Susannah Stacey

Mushroom Sauce

Take a piece of butter rolled in flour, stir in your stewpan till the flour is of a fine yellow colour; then put in some stock, a glass of white wine, a bundle of parsley, thyme, laurel, and sweet basil, two cloves, some nutmeg or mace, a few mushrooms, pepper and salt. Let it stew an hour over a slow fire, then skim all the fat clean off, and strain it through a lawn sieve.

Susannah Stacey

Mushrooms in Cream

Arrange eight large, firm caps, gill side up, or one pound of small mushrooms in a shallow, buttered pan; sprinkle with salt and pepper and dot with butter. Add about half a cup of cream and bake for ten minutes in a hot oven. Place the caps on pieces of toast and just before serving pour over them cream remaining in the pan.

Breakfast Puffballs

Gather puffballs immediately the white spheres are glimsped in the grass, skin them and cut them in half inch slices. Fry them in a little fat to serve with bacon and egg.

A PUNNET OF MIXED FRUIT

West Tarring, a quaint old flinty village now enveloped by Worthing, is noted for its fig garden. Thomas a Becket is said to have planted the original tree, or seed, having brought it back from his mission to Rome. As Archbishop of Canterbury, he would no doubt have visited Tarring, which had been granted to the see of Canterbury by King Athelstan in the tenth century. Another tradition says that it was Saint Richard, Bishop of Chichester, who planted the fig trees when he was living in Tarring Rectory with the priest, Simon de Terring, in the thirteenth century.

What is certain is that in 1745 a fig orchard was planted at Bishops Garth with cuttings from the archbishop's palace garden. Within 100 years there were 100 trees producing 2,000 figs annually, and the orchard was laid out with paths so the gentry from Worthing could walk around it.

Over the years the number of trees increased to a peak of some 200 by the 1950s. Today about 120 remain. Two houses have been built in the fig garden, reducing its size by about one third. The fig orchard is now divided between the two new houses and Bishops Garth and the three owners have an open day once a year – usually the first Saturday in July.

A substantial glasshouse industry developed in the Worthing area and, with the arrival of the railway, hot house grapes, tomatoes, melons, strawberries, figs and nectarines were despatched to Brighton and London. By the the turn of the century more than 600 tons of fruit a year was leaving Worthing, much of it for Leeds, Birmingham, Manchester and Glasgow.

The decline in this trade began with the First World War when the glasshouses went over to producing vegetables. Between the wars tomatoes were the main crop, but the Second World War again saw mass production of vegetables. After the war much of the land was sold for residential development and by 1976 an industry which had employed around 1,500 men had been reduced to only ten acres of glasshouses.

The famous Californian seedless raisin originated in Mayfield, according to another Sussex legend. Many, many years ago, so the story goes, three cuttings from a Mayfield vine were sent to a Sussex settler in California. Two were well tended, but were destroyed by flood. The settler turned to the neglected third vine which, to his amazement, he found bore seedless fruit. From this one plant the entire Californian industry grew.

Marjorie Hessell Tiltman quotes her daily woman, Mrs Hickman, on the subject of prunes. 'Up at the House they was allus askin' me for prune fritters – soak' em as usual, stone 'em, halve 'em, dip 'em in batter just the same as for apples or bananas, and quickfry 'em in deep fat. No, there ain't no call to be dull with prunes, what with prune mousse, and prune tart and prune jelly. And then, about September, we'd lay down some prunes in gin, to have about Christmastide. My, they ate up something grand, after a heavy dinner like. And then there's prunes rolled in tiny bits o' grilled bacon for savouries, and veal stuffed with prunes and apples – you can go pretty well through a whole dinner with prunes knockin' your elbow.'

Nature's larder in Sussex is well stocked with 'fruits for free' – wild white raspberries on the Downs above Firle, tiny wild strawberries in the woods at Stanmer (for a fine tea, gather the strawberry leaves in spring, when they are young, and dry them in the air, but out of the sun, then infuse the tea in the manner of Chinese green tea), whortleberries on Ashdown Forest, sloes (for sloe gin), bullaces and wild plums (for jams and jellies) in the hedgerows, wild crabs (for jellies and pickles) in country lanes, elderberries for jellies and wines, sweet chestnuts and cobs in ancient woods, and blackberries everywhere, even in the towns and on the roadside verges.

As in other counties, there are dire warnings for those who pick and eat blackberries after a certain date. In Sussex the date is

October 10, which is the day when the Devil spits on all the bushes, marking the fruit as his own.

Going blackberrying is no longer the occasion it was when whole families, including uncles, aunts and cousins, would take a picnic on the Downs, with many basins, baskets and punnets, and return weary, scratched but triumphant in the evening  with pounds and pounds of luscious blackberries to transform into jellies, cordials, puddings and tarts and, of course, blackberry and apple jam.

The county was once renowned for the the quality of its apples. The Golden Pippin was first grown at Plumpton Place by Leonard Mascall, who discovered it in France around 1571, and it was exported to Russia for Catherine the Great, each fruit wrapped in gold tinted paper, which is how it came by its name.

The Swiss used to prize another locally grown apple, the Five Crowns of Sussex, and there were the Alfriston Pippin, said to be a superior cooking apple to the Bramley Seedling, the Gooseberry Knock-out, the Nanny, the Forge, the Sussex Ducksbill, the Sussex Greenlanes, the Wadhurst Pippin and many, many more, now all lost except for the occasional gnarled old tree in a country garden.

Apple trees were called pippins because they were grown from pips, it being a crime in the sixteenth century to bark an apple tree. The staple apple before the introduction of pippins from Europe was the costard and apple sellers were known as costard mongers.

Apple jelly with chopped mint is a fine accompaniment for roast lamb; with chopped sage for roast pork and with lemon, or elderberries (in a muslin bag, as for a bouquet garni) for game and poultry.

Oringe Fretters

Grate three or four oringes in a pint of cream or good milk, five or six eggs, thicken it with flour of a good thickness and Fry them that they may be dry. With this Batter you may make fretters with slices of Aples. *Arundel ms*

Wax Basket for Confectionery

Melt together over the fire half a pound of white wax, a quarter of a pound of spermaceti, half an ounce of flake white, and a quarter of an ounce of hog's lard. Oil a basket mould; and then, the melted wax not being too hot, run it round the inside. When cool, take the basket out of the mould, and ornament it with coloured wax Wax baskets are sometimes painted in oil colours with landscapes or figures; and they are, also, often adorned with flowers, fruit, etc.
Susannah Stacey

To Make a Hasty Pudding in a Bagg

Take thick creame and boyle it with three spoonfulls of flower; season it wth sugar, nutmeg and sault; then turn your bagg the inside outward and strow it wth flower, then power in your creame being hott into your bagg, and lett your water seeth before you putt it in, and when it is enough put it into a dish and putt butter on it in many places, and if it bee well made it will cutt like a custard.
Early eighteenth century Mark Cross ms

Rhubarb Mousse

Stew the rhubarb (which can be old and tough) gently with a little brown sugar and no water and a pinch of ground ginger and a spoonful of chopped, crystallised ginger. Whip the yolk of an egg and mix with the rhubarb. Mix the white very stiffly and fold into the rhubarb mixture. Turn into an oven proof dish and bake for a few minutes.
West Sussex family recipe, nineteenth century

Strawberry Fritters

To two eggs well beat, whites and yolks both, put about half a pint of cream, made thick with fine flour, a little fine sugar and nutmeg, put your strawberries in raw, and fry them in a pan of clean lard, a spoonful at a time, dish them up in a pyramid, and sift sugar between and at top. This is a pretty way of making fritters with any sort of fruit.
William Verral

Rice and Apple Pudding

Boil a quarter of a pound of rice in milk till it is very tender and let it be as thick as you can stir it, add to it one egg, a few spoonfuls of cream, nutmeg and sugar to your taste. Then pare and core your apples, put them in a dish, pour over the rice and bake for half an hour. Serve with a butter and wine sauce.

Cowslip Pudding

Cut and pound the flowers of a peck of cowslips, half a pound of Naples biscuit grated, and three pints of cream. Boil them a little, then beat up sixteen eggs, with a little rose-water sweetened. Mix all togeher, butter a dish, and pour it in. Bake it; and, when done, sift fine sugar over, and serve it up hot.

Susannah Stacey

Quince Pudding

Scald your quinces tender, pare them thin, scrape off the pulp, mix with sugar very sweet, and add a little ginger and cinnamon. To a pint of cream you must put three or four yolks of eggs, and stir it into your quinces till they are of a good thickness. Butter your dish, pour it in, and bake it.

Chestnut Pudding

Boil a dozen and a half of chestnuts a quarter of an hour. Blanch, peel and beat them in a marble mortar, with a little orange-flower or rose water, and white wine, till of a fine thin paste. Beat up twelve eggs with the whites. Grate half a nutmeg into three pints of cream, a little salt, and half a pound of melted butter. Sweeten it, and mix all together. Put it over the fire, and stir it till thick. Lay a puff paste over the dish, pour the mixture, and send it to the oven.

Susannah Stacey

Snow Balls

Pare and take the cores out of five large baking apples, and fill the holes with orange or quince marmalade. Make some good hot paste, roll your apples in it, and make your crust of equal thickness. Put them in a tin dripping pan, bake them in a moderate oven, and when you take them out, make icing for them. Let your icing be about a quarter of an inch thick, and set them at a good distance from the fire till hardened; but do not let them brown.

(Susannah Stacey made icing with a pound of double-refined sugar and the whites of twenty four eggs, with orange-flower water and fresh lemon peel to give flavour. It was whisked for three hours then, in the case of the Snow Balls, spread over them and left in a warm place to harden).

Five Minute Pudding

Mix together three tablespoons of flour, three dessertspoons of sugar, one dessertspoon of baking powder and two eggs. Spread it in a buttered tin, bake five minutes then spread with jam and roll up. Serve with custard.

Sussex Cream

Take one pint of milk, four eggs, one ounce of gelatine, half a wineglassful of sherry, five ounces of sugar, a quarter of a pound of macaroons, glace cherries, half an orange and cream. Soak the gelatine in cold milk. Boil the milk and add the yolks of eggs, the grated rind of the orange, the sugar and the macaroons. Stir it all the time until it thickens, then add the gelatine and sherry. Strain it and cool. Add the cream and the cherries. Pour it into a wetted mould. Turn it out when set and serve it on a silver dish.

Brandy Pudding

Line a mould with jar raisins stoned, or dried cherries, then thin slices of French roll, next ratifias, or macaroons, then fruit, then roll, and so on till the mould is filled. Sprinkle in at times two glasses of brandy. Beat four eggs; put to a pint of milk or cream, sweetened and a grating of nutmeg. Let the liquid sink into the solid part, tie it tight in a cloth, and boil it one hour.
Susannah Stacey

Poor Curate's Pudding

Rub a few bread crumbs, pare and slice a few apples, put a layer of apples and a layer of bread crumbs, flavour it with nutmeg and sweeten it to your taste, pour over the top a little clarified butter and bake it in a quick oven.
Ellen Shoosmith 1850

A Fine Syllabub from the Cow

Sweeten a quart of cyder with refined sugar, grate a nutmeg over it; and milk the cow into your liquor. When you have added what is necessary, pour half a pint of the sweetest cream over it.
Barbara Young, Steyning 1781

Honeycomb Cream

Put into a glass dish or china bowl, the juice of two lemons, one glass of sherry, half a glass of brandy, two large tablespoons of sugar and grate a little nutmeg over. Put a quart of cream in a saucepan with a piece of lemon peel and about eight lumps of sugar, let it boil ten minutes, then pour it into a jug (removing lemon peel). Place the dish on the floor and, standing on a chair, pour the heated cream into the other ingredients from as great a height as you can conveniently. It should be made the day before it is wanted.

Mrs Gillow 1761–1831

Sussex Strawberry Pudding

Cook one pound of strawberries with a quarter of a pound of castor sugar in half a pint of water until soft, then rub through a sieve. Add half an ounce of gelatine and one and a half ounces of sugar to a pint of milk and bring it to the boil. Stir until the gelatine has dissolved. Strain into a jug. Put the fruit pulp into a glass dish and pour the milk over just before it sets. Serve cold.

A Dish of Snow

Put twelve apples over the fire in cold water till soft, then put them on a sieve; skin and put the pulp in a basin; beat up the whites of twelve eggs to a froth, then sift half a pound of double refined sugar and strew it in the eggs; beat the pulp to a froth, then beat the whole together till like stiff snow. Heap it high on a china dish, stick a sprig of myrtle in the middle, and serve it up.

Susannah Stacey

Potato Pudding Very Good

Take two pounds of white Potatoes, boil and peel them, and beat them in a morter so small, as not to be discover'd what they are; then take half a pound of Butter and mix it with ye yolks of eight eggs and the white of three; beat them very well, and mix in a pint of Cream and half a pint of sack, a pound of refin'd sugar with a little salt and spice, and Bake it.

Arundel ms

Blackcurrant Leaf Sorbet

Boil up some syrup with half a pound of sugar and a pint of water, put in a handful of young blackcurrant leaves, cover, cool, strain and add the juice of six lemons. Freeze the mixture, and when starting to set, stir it and freeze it again. Serve with cream.

To Make Lemon Creame my Cousin Sue Harres Way

Take three pints of creame and boyle it, then keepe it stirring till it be but blood warm, then take the meat of three lemons and stir them well with sugar and strain it and put to it two spoonfull of rose water or oringe flower water, then put it to the cream and stir it very well together and put into custard pans.

Ann Lord

Pain Perdu

Boil three pints of milk, two handfuls of loaf sugar, one stick of vanilla for two or three hours until quite a thick syrup, almost like condensed milk. Pour over rounds of bread, cut almost an inch thick. Let them soak well then dip in a mixture of beaten eggs and castor sugar. Fry quickly in a pan of hot butter until nicely browned both sides. Serve hot with hot golden syrup and whipped cream.

Lady Gage

Brass and iron scales and weights, c 1890

BREAD, CAKES AND BISCUITS

Today bread is inexpensive, plentiful and available in such variety that it hardly seems worth the effort of all that kneading and proving to produce a loaf heavy as a house brick and as digestible. Indeed, the product of many amateur bakers is similar to bread made in the Middle Ages. This was so dense and hard that it was sliced and used as plates, or trenchers, becoming digestible only when impregnated with the fats, juices and flavours of the meal. In grand houses bread trenchers were saved for the servants' meal – this, often, being all they had to eat.

Although bakeries have been in existence for centuries it was not always considered prudent to buy their wares. The pioneering cook and food writer Eliza Acton, born 1799, the daughter of a Battle brewer, condemned them as filthy, unhygienic sweatshops, producing bad bread.

The infamous Corn Laws had much to answer for. They were implemented to protect farmers from imported grain and to keep home grown wheat prices stable. The farmers, though, adopted the habit of hoarding part of their harvest from one year to the next, to act as a buffer should there be a wet summer and a poor yield. Often the stored grain rotted, yet still it was sold, at the guaranteed price, and the result was bread that was virtually unfit for consumption.

The bakers were as devious as the farmers, many adulterating the flour with alum, chalk, Plaster of Paris, magnesium, ammonia carbonate, potato and even pipe clay. The really poor, those without bread ovens in their cottages, and the labouring classes in the towns, relied on the baker for their daily bread, the cheapest food available to them. Too often they were cheated and not infrequently poisoned by the baker.

Large houses had their own bake houses; in every farmhouse kitchen there was a great brick oven, six feet or more deep; and a smaller bread oven was built into many of the farmworker's cottages.

On baking day, weekly or fortnightly, according to the size of the household, a quantity of shavings was laid in the brick oven with small branches, hazel faggots or gorse on top. Then a shaving of wood was dipped in brimstone, set alight with a tinder and applied to the faggots. As the fire caught more faggots were piled in followed by logs of cord wood. A long handled iron peel was used to spread the fire to every part of the oven then the iron door was secured and the fire allowed to burn for around two hours, or until it was judged hot enough for baking.

Very quickly, so as to conserve the heat in the bricks, the glowing embers were shovelled out and a bundle of green broom dipped in water was used to sweep the oven floor clean. Then the loaves, up to twenty or so, already mixed, kneaded and proved, were put inside and while they were baking rolls, pies and tarts were prepared to take their place in the oven when the bread came out.

As the oven cooled, cakes, rice and tapioca puddings went in and finally jars of seasonal fruit for preserving. On some farms, if any heat remained, feathers for feather beds went in to be sterilised.

Bread Chips

Cut thin shavings of bread from a stale loaf, spread them on a dish, or lay them singly on the tin tray of an American oven, and dry them very gradually until they are perfectly crisp; then bring them to a pale straw colour; withdraw them from the fire, and, as soon as they are cold, pile them on a napkin, and serve them without delay. They require an extremely gentle oven to produce the propper effect on them; but, if well managed, will retain their crispness for several hours; and it may also be renewed by heating them through afresh.

Eliza Acton

Crusts to Serve with Cheese

Take a half baked loaf from the oven and tear it into small rough bits with a couple of forks; lay these on a tin, and put them back into the oven for ten minutes. If a light loaf be made for the purpose, with new milk and two ounces of butter, they will quite resemble rusks. A sweet like cake pulled apart in the same manner is likewise very good.

Eliza Acton

Of all the eleven English counties where gingerbread was made and sold in the eighteenth and nineteenth centuries, Sussex claimed to have the best – and it came from Horsham.

At every fair there was a stall selling gingerbread fairings – with the sweetmeat in the shape of Wellington on horseback, the Royal Coat of Arms, cats, a grandfather clock and the Prince of Wales's feathers. Often the designs were picked out in shining gold icing – the gilt on the gingerbread.

A man called Mansbridge, who had a shop in The Square at Westbourne, became so rich from his sought after gingerbread that in 1840 he retired to a farm at Prinsted which he called Gingerbread Farm. He had a rival, a Mr Poate, also of Westbourne and between the two competition was fierce to see who could produce the best designs for

Gingerbread cutter

the five annual fairs at Horsham. The largest, in July, lasted for a week and a day.

Sussex had three types of gingerbread. There was Hard which was rich, dark brown and made with black treacle; Toy, made with light treacle; and Parliament, a thin, crisp biscuit used for fancy shapes.

Hard Gingerbread

Mix together two pounds of flour, half a pound of coarse sugar, one large spoon of carbonate of soda and one ounce of powdered ginger. Melt half a pound of lard in half a pint of milk, add one pound of black treacle, mix this with the dry ingredients then spread in a shallow, greased baking tray. Bake in a slow oven for 45 minutes.

Toy Gingerbread

Beat six ounces of butter and six ounces of caster sugar to a cream. Add three eggs and three ounces of light treacle (golden syrup), then half a pound of sifted flour, a teaspoon of mixed spice, a teaspoon of ground ginger, a pinch of baking powder and four ounces of shredded almonds. Pour the mixture into a greased and papered baking tin and cook for 45 minutes in a moderate oven.

Parliament Gingerbread

Mix half a pound of flour, two ounces of bicarbonate of soda, a teaspoon of ground ginger and two ounces of ground caraway with enough golden syrup to make a very stiff dough. Roll out the dough into long, very thin sheets and cut out with an appropriate biscuit cutter. Place on a slightly greased baking sheet, splash with water, and bake in a slow oven until crisp and golden.

To Make Ginger Bread

Take a pound of flower strow in an ounce of betten ginger and a pound of sugar, then mince very fine ye Rinds of 4 Civill oranges and put into yr flower, then warme 3 pound of shopp surrop and power in ye midle, so work it up to a past and rowle it pritty thinn and cutt it with a glase into cakes and so bake it.

Arundel ms

Almond Bisket

Take half a pound of Almonds, blanch and beat them in a mortar with ye froth of six whites of eggs, put in by degrees, then beat in scarce a pound of Double refined sugar, mix it up with ye yolks of ye six eggs, strow in a quarter of a pound of dryed flower and ye peel of two large lemons grated, beat them all together very well with the almonds and bake them in a quick oven. Paper coffins will doe, but Tin pans better.

Arundel ms

Windmill Hill Thin Biscuits

Two handsful of flour, a little pinch of salt, butter about the size of a walnut, half a small teaspoonful of baking powder. Rub all well together, add milk to make a stiff paste. Roll out very thin and bake.

Sussex Girdle Cakes

Take three ounces of fresh butter and set it before the fire to melt; when melted, add to it rather more than quarter of a pint of new milk and mix one pound of flour well with it; work it till it becomes rather stiff and roll it out to the thickness of a little less than quarter of an inch. The girdle must be put on the fire before the cake is ready that it may be well heated. The above is the proper quantity for a girdle measuring fifteen inches in diameter. This cake will require twenty minutes to bake. It should be cut into small oblong pieces after it is baked and then sliced open and a small piece of fresh butter put into each bit. If liked, a few currants may be added before it is baked.

Much appreciated by children in earlier times were Sussex Plum Heavies – small round fruity cakes made from the pasty left over from the weekly baking. When Dr J C Sanger of Seaford was sent to the Cape of Good Hope as Government Surgeon in the 1870s he was called to the home of an English settler and found the family at the tea table.

'You come from Sussex,' the doctor declared.

'Yes, from Horsemouncies (Herstmonceux),' was the answer. 'But how did you know?'

'Because you have plum heavies for tea which I never saw but when I have been visiting in Sussex,' said the doctor.

Plum Heavies

Add a handful of raisins or currants to ordinary pie crust pastry. Flatten between the palms and bake on a tray until golden brown. Sometimes sugar was added and sometimes raised pie pastry was used. This was made by adding boiling hot fat – brisket fat was considered superior – to the dry ingredients and the dough rolled out and cut into rings or squares.

To Make Wallnutt Cakes

Take half a pound of Wallnutts after they are blanch, beat them very well in a marble morter with a little orange flower water then have ye whites of two eggs well beaten, put them in with two spoonfulls of very fine flower and half a pound of double refine sugar beaten and sifted. Put them all together and beat them till just they goe into ye oven, then drop them upon tinn sheets butter'd.

Arundel ms

To Make a Cake my Lady Ashburnham's Way

Take half a peck of fine flower, break into it a pound of sweet butter. Strow into it a quarter of a pound of fine white sugar, to nutmeges and a little mace finely beaten, fower pound of corrants washed and rubed, a pint of good ale yeast, 6 eggs whits and yolckes well beaten. A quart of cream. Mingle all these together and let it stand by the fier half an houre, then turn it out on a thick paper. Strew sum flower one it and clap it down with your hand. Three quarters of an hour is inough to bake it. You must butter the paper that goes round it.

Ann Lord

Hove resident Lady Strathspey claimed, in 1942, that the original recipe for the Bath Bun was in Brighton. 'It was given, or so the legend goes,' she said, 'as part of the dowry of Miss Fort, daughter of the renowned Bath baker, when she married the founder of a Brighton bakery, well known to several generations of Brighton citizens'. When the bakery eventually closed the recipe became part of the lease of the establishment, apparently. Mr Fort's recipe remains a secret to this day, but here is a Sussex version used at East Chiltington in the mid nineteenth century.

Brighton Bath Bun

Take one pound of flour, the rinds of three lemons, grated fine, half a pound of butter melted in a coffee cup of cream, a teaspoonful of yeast and five eggs. Add one pound of powdered loaf sugar. Work well. Let it stand to rise, and it will make thirty-nine Bath buns.

Susannah Stacey

Brighton Sandwich

Grease an eight inch cake tin and line with greased paper. In a bowl mix together eight ounces self raising flour, one ounce semolina and four ounces castor sugar. Rub in four ounces of butter, add a beaten egg and bind together. Divide the mixture and roll out one half to fit into the tin. Spread jam in the centre. Roll out the second half and place on top. Cover with split almonds. Bake the cake in a medium oven for 15 minutes then reduce heat for a further 20 minutes.

FOOD FOR THE POOR

KETTLE bender, kettle broth, brewis, potluck – these were all names for a frugal dish common across the county in the 1840s and for many years afterwards. It was made by filling a basin with pieces of bread, pouring on boiling water, or the liquor in which meat or vegetables had been boiled, and adding a knob of butter, or dripping, pepper and salt. On winter mornings children were better able to face the walk to school with a basinful of bender inside. Often kettle bender was all a poor family had for supper, and it was also a comforting dish for those who felt queasy.

When circumstances permitted, odds and ends of cheese were mixed with the bread, and the resulting broth would spoon up like toffee – or a chopped raw onion was stirred in. In some homes cocoa powder and sugar replaced pepper and salt to make a coloured cousin to bread and milk.

A particularly rough time for the poor followed the wet summer of 1860 when few fields could be harvested and hay was in such short supply the following winter that cattle were fed on thatch from the barns. The flour was so bad that bread would not bake properly and the middle had to be scooped out with a spoon. Many families went hungry that year.

In those days it was customary in many well-to-do homes to set aside food for the poor – and even to have the cook make special dishes for the needy.

Good, nourishing soups were popular, especially with the givers, for quite often the cost was nil. Scraps from the dining table and from the servants' hall were collected. In the kitchen, bones and fish heads were saved and, together with a few vegetables and perhaps some left over gravy, the whole lot was simmered to make a substantial broth.

Alice Catherine Day, in her book *Glimpses of Rural Life in Sussex,* looked back to the hard times on the land in the 1850s. Her mother, who ran a farm at Hadlow Down, could not afford to increase the workers' wages. Instead she asked the men how she could help them over the coming winter.

'Well, Madam, we have been talking it over, and made up our minds to ask you if we can have nice soup, such as you have given us from time to time, provided twice a week,' they said.

A large copper was acquired, flour, rice and oatmeal bought by the hundredweight, neighbours sent vegetables to supplement those grown on the farm, and the butcher was liberal. For an outlay of £25 soup was made and distributed at the rate of a quart each, twice a week, to every member of the labourers' families. Children on their way home from school took cans to be filled. If any remained after the farm workers had been served, outsiders were able to buy the soup for one penny per quart. The distribution lasted over five months.

Cheap Soup for Poor People

Two ozs dripping; half lb solid meat at 4d per lb, cut into dice one inch square; quarter lb onions sliced thin; two ozs leeks (green tops will do); quarter lb turnips cut into dice; three ozs celery chopped small – 1d; half lb rice or pearl barley – 1d; three ozs salt and quarter lb brown sugar; six quarts water. Fuel to make it – fid. The whole to cost 6d.

Take an iron saucepan (a tin one will not do), put into it over the fire your meat cut small with the dripping and the brown sugar, shred in your onions. Stir with a wooden spoon till fried lightly brown. Add your turnips, celery and leeks, stir about ten minutes. Add one quart cold water and your barley or rice. Mix well together. Add five quarts hot water, season with salt and stir occasionally till boiling. Then let it simmer on the hob for three hours, when the barley will be tender. This soup will keep for two or three days if poured into a flat pan. Stir till nearly cold when taken off the fire, which will prevent it fermenting. *Mrs Gould*

Thomas Turner was taken with a similar recipe for a cheap and nourishing soup he came across in *The Universal Magazine of Knowledge and Pleasure* in December 1758. Having sampled it, he recommended it highly to his card playing and drinking companions, and he copied it out verbatim in his diary.

Universal Soup

Take half a pound of beef, mutton, or pork, cut into small pieces; half a pint of peas, three sliced turnips, and three potatoes cut very small, an onion or two, or a few leeks; put to them three quarts and a pint of water; let it boil gently on a very slow fire about two hours and an half, then thicken it with a quarter of a pound of ground rice, and half a quarter of a pound of oatmeal (or a quarter of a pound of oatmeal and no rice); boil it for a quarter of an hour after the thickening is put in stirring it all the time; then season it with salt, ground pepper or pounded ginger to your taste.

Caudle for the Poor When Sick or Lying In

Put three quarts of water on the fire; mix smooth in cold water some oatmeal to thicken it; when boiling, pour the latter in, and twenty powdered Jamaica peppers; boil to a good middling thickness; then add sugar, half a pint of well fermented table beer, and a glass of gin. Boil all together. The above caudle given once or twice, with a nourishing broth as often, would, indeed, be doing a great charity.

Susannah Stacey

Broth

Boil a pound of good beef or mutton in six quarts of water and with three ounces of Scotch barley. After it has boiled some time, put in a mixture made from an ounce of oatmeal and a little cold water. Stir well and add a handful of chopped onions, chives, parsley and thyme.

In some rural communities village clubs or benefit societies were formed. Members paid a few pence a month and in return were entitled to a small allowance when they were sick or too old to work. Few were successful. Club meetings often took place in the pub and funds, instead of being deposited, were spent on drink for club officers, or a good dinner at Christmas. Rules about working while receiving the allowance were strict; one man was expelled from his club because he put a couple of sticks on the fire by which he was sitting.

A hard pudding was a good standby when times were rough. This was made by mixing a pound of plain flour with half a pint of water to a light dough which was formed into dumplings and left in a warm place for several hours. The dumplings were then dropped into boiling water for thirty minutes and eaten in a soup or broth if any were available, or on their own with a sprinkling of salt and pepper, hog fat or butter.

Hedgehogs were once eaten in Sussex. Usually the bristles were shaved off and the animal was split open from nose to tail and baked. It tasted not unlike pork and produced a fine crackling. Gypsies would gut the hedgehog, wrap it in clay and put it on the fire. When the clay was broken open the spikes came out with it, leaving tender pink meat.

Desperate fathers went poaching to stave off starvation, driven by hungry children to risk Draconian penalties if caught. The women went leasing, or gleaning, scrabbling for grains in the fields after the harvest.

The Battle in the Carnfield in the Hungry Forties was recounted almost 100 years later by Mrs Jolly, a bedridden old woman living near Midhurst. It was told to her by her mother who took part in the battle.

In each parish the women had the right to go gleaning in their own fields, but on one large field the three parishes of Ironwood, Didstead and Elham met. The Ironwood women had always had the gleaning rights in the field but one afternoon women from the other parishes arrived to search for grain.

'Who be you to come leasing 'long of us?' the Ironwood women demanded. The interlopers were told to leave but 't'other women said they weren't gwine home, they were gwine to goo on leasing, for they and their chillun was as hungry as anyone else and p'raps more. And then they all went on a-nabbling and a-quarelling and arguing till a Miss Pett, from Didstead – oh, a lil tiny puny woman she was, Mother said, with a white face – lashed out and about, she did and slapped up at an Ironwood woman, my mother's cousin she was, Nancy Marriner by name, a gurt ox of a woman, more like a man in her size and ways, with big hands and feet on her.

'Miss Pett she just up and slapped her face hard and then Nancy Marriner she caught hold of Miss Pett round her middle, she did, and swung her off her feet, and Miss Pett she held on to Nancy's right ear good an' hard an' she swung an' she pulled with all her strength and off come the earring, crash – right out of Nancy Marriner's ear and brought a bit o' flesh and a smart lot of blood with it.

'Nancy Marriner she slawed hold of Miss Pett's bonnet and hair and was a-tearing away like a lion at 'em when someone hollered close to 'em in a roaring kind of voice: "Goo it! Goo it! I backs the lil one from Didstead!" and if there warn't the farmer the field belonged to, yaas! Farmer Cobden!'

Mrs Jolly's grandmother had only one shilling and sixpence and a loaf of bread to live on each week and her daughter, Mrs Jolly's mother, used to save scraps – 'and p'raps a lil mess of pea shucks boiled' and take them to her.

'But she had to do it quiet, for when my Father found out he'd swear and knock her about crool. Oh, a crool, greedy man he were – but Mother she kept on all the same whenever she could.'

The children themselves did their best to put food on the table by catching wild creatures. Sparrows nesting under the eaves of thatched cottages were poked out with a stick and trapped in deep nets. Catapults, snares and wires were used to kill pheasants, blackbirds and thrushes. For a pie big enough for the average family two dozen blackbirds were needed – hence the rhyme 'Four and Twenty Blackbirds.

In the country round Battle a favourite occupation was scug hunting – knocking squirrels out of trees with a special stick which was weighted at one end so that it would drop back down after it had been thrown.

THE FESTIVE YEAR

'It's six o'clock on a Christmas morn.
Mistresses arise and let your maids lie still
For they have risen all the year,
Much against their wills'.

Lewes town cry

PREPARATIONS for Christmas used to begin in Sussex on Stir-up Sunday – the Sunday before Advent – when, in church, the Collect for the day began 'Stir up, we beseech thee, O Lord'. This was the signal for housewives to stir up their puddings and mince-meat, and for grocers to dress their shop windows with Christmas fruits and spices.

In castles and country seats the Twelve Days of Christmas were celebrated at tables groaning with roast swan, geese, venison, roast boar, capons, pike and larks. There were extravagant cakes and exotic fruits in syrup, countless barrels of beer and bottles of wine. This outrageous consumption moderated in the Victorian era, although even then the Christmas board would still be considered excessive by modern standards.

Ray Silver writing in 1943, describes a Sussex farmhouse Christmas of fifty years earlier. 'The old brick oven has been doing double duty in baking bread, pies and cakes. . . the hams have been inspected and the best selected and boiled in the large cauldron on the pot hangers over the log fire. The pig has been killed and dressed, and that which was not required fresh, salted down for future use.

'On Christmas day the glazed and decorated boar's head on its pewter platter takes pride of position in the centre of the old oak dresser. The roast beef in the charge of father, after thanks has been given, is served to the resident family and those who have returned to join in the festivities, followed by the huge Christmas pudding with the holly crown and flame licked sides and mince pies under the able supervision of mother. Copious drinks with nuts and fruit, the remembrance of absent friends, all add to the fulfilment of the old customs.'

One more ritual was observed at the end of the festivities. 'The burning of the yule log will continue each day until Twelfth Night when the last piece will be placed on one side to be stored until the next yule log takes its place. So shall good luck attend this house during the ensuing year.'

In the old days mincemeat really was minced meat. Before Cromwell banned the observance of Christmas, mince pies were oblong with rounded corners – the shape of Jesus's manger, with a concave top crust in which a Christ figure of dough was placed. The rich, sweet, spiced filling represented the gifts given by the Three Wise Men.

It was the custom for families to go from house to house, sampling each other's mince pies. For every pie eaten, a happy month would follow. Some attached the same superstition to Christmas pudding – that a lucky month would follow for each different pudding tasted. Another way of making sure the coming year would be trouble free was to keep a small piece of the Christmas cake until another was made a year later.

The traditional Christmas pudding recipe used today is only a little more than 200 years old. Its predecessor was plumb pottage, a heavily fruited and spiced meat dish, of a porridge consistency. And the predecessor of plumb pottage was frumenty, hulled wheat spiced and boiled in milk. Such additions as eggs, dried prunes and pieces of meat were added to this over many years until it became the pottage, served in a tureen.

Where Christmas puddings are still made at home today, the tradition of stirring with a wooden spoon and making a wish is sometimes followed. This derives from a custom attached to the making of plumb pottage. The spoon had to be wooden because the manger was made of wood, and the stirring had to be from left to right or disaster would strike the household. In Victorian times the Christmas pudding was first stirred by the mother, then the father, followed by the children in order of age, then the domestic servants.

Not every home had facilities for cooking a roast Christmas dinner and housewives were often dependent on the local baker who turned over his ovens to his customers. Veteran author and folk singer Bob Copper recalls the year he and his brother set out from their Rottingdean cottage home to fetch the turkey and a joint of beef that had been roasted in Mr Hilder's bakery along with those of other villagers.

The women of the family were at home preparing the vegetables, the sauces and the trimmings for the arrival of the grand centrepiece. Carrying this succulent load between them on a stretcher the boys decided, as they passed the frozen pond, to enliven their task by sliding across the ice.

'Suddenly there was a fusillade of sound like rifle fire and I dropped through the ice and stood knee deep in freezing water' said Bob. The stretcher slanted and the two dishes started to slide towards a watery grave but they were saved by his quick witted brother sinking down in the mud to restore the stretcher to an even keel.

In country homes the wassail (from the Anglo Saxon *waes hael*, be well) bowl was always made at Christmas time. It was made with hot ale, nutmeg and roasted apples, although sometimes wine was used instead of ale. Traditionally the bowl was placed on a small round table and those present were each given a silver spoon. They walked round the table, singing and stirring the liquid with the right hand as they went.

Wassailing, a practice which died out in the Sussex orchards around the turn of the century, dates back more than a thousand years. Any time between Christmas Eve and Twelfth Night farm workers and village boys, one with a cow's horn to trumpet their arrival, would whack the apple trees in the orchards with sticks to ensure a good crop and chant wassail verses, of which there were many local variations.

Royal Pyes

Make pastry with eight ounces of plain flour, two ounces of butter, two ounces of sugar and an egg yolk. Line tart tins with the thinly rolled pastry and bake blind for fifteen minutes. Mix three quarters of an ounce of butter with the rind and juice of one lemon, eight ounces of mincemeat, two egg yolks and a tablespoon of rum or brandy. Fill the pastry tarts and top with a meringue made from two egg whites and four ounces of caster sugar. Bake for thirty minutes in a medium oven until meringue is crisp.

Sussex Spiced Beef

Take 12 pounds of round of beef and rub it well all over with coarse brown sugar; leave it for two days. Mix together one ounce saltpetre, six ounces salt, two ounces pepper, one ounce allspice, two ounces crushed juniper berries. With this mixture rub the beef each morning for a fortnight, turning the round each day, and rubbing for about ten minutes each time. At the end of the fortnight wash off the spice and put the beef into an earthen pan, as near its own size as possible, with half a pint of water. Cover the top of the beef with a thick layer of chopped suet and over the pan put a crust made from one pound of flour and two ounces of lard mixed with water and rolled out thickly. Cover the pan and bake in a moderate oven for four hours. Let the beef get cold in the pan then remove the crust and the suet and turn out the beef. Serve cold. This will keep for two or three weeks.

Updated from an 18th century recipe by Jennifer Jane 1930

Plumb Pottage

Take of beef-soup made of legs of beef, 12 quarts; if you wish it to be particularly good, add a couple of tongues to be boiled therein. Put fine bread, sliced, soaked and crumbled; raisins of the sun, currants and pruants two lbs. of each; lemons, nutmegs, mace and cloves are to be boiled with it in a muslin bag; add a quart of red wine and let this be followed, after half an hour's boiling, by a pint of sack. Put it into a cool place and it will keep through Christmas.

Eighteenth century Sussex recipe

Granny's Plum Pudding

Two pounds of currants, three quarters of a pound of soft brown sugar, two pounds of raisins, six ounces mixed peel, two pounds of beef suet, grated rind of half a lemon, one and a half pounds breadcrumbs, one teaspoon mixed spice, one and a half pounds flour, six bitter almonds blanched and chopped, three quarters of a pound of treacle, half a nutmeg grated, one bottle of stout. Mix all the ingrdients then add the treacle and the stout, divide into puddings and boil for ten hours

Jennifer Jane 1930

Christmas Plum Pudding

If you wish to make a pudding in which everyone delights
Of six pretty new-laid eggs you must take the yolks and whites.
Take a pound of well- stoned raisins and a pound of currants dried.
A pound of pounded sugar and some candied peel besides.
Take a pound of well- choopped suet and a pound of wheaten flour,
And let them stand to settle for a quarter of an hour.
Mix them all up together till they thoroughly combine,
And be sure you chop the suet up particularly fine.
Then put the mixture in a cloth and put it in the pot;
Some people like the water cold and some prefer it hot.
But as I don't know which of the two I ought to praise,
I know I ought to boil an hour for every pound it weighs.
OH! If I were Queen of France, or still better, Pope of Rome,
I'd have a Christmas pudding every day I dined at home.
All the world should have a piece, and if any should remain,
Next morning for my breakfast I would have it fried again.

Sussex recipe from the 19th century in song form

Mincemeat

A pound and a quarter of meat (tongue is best) two pounds and a half of suet, three quarters of a pound of raisins, all chopped fine, three pounds of currants. Mace, cloves, cinnamon and nutmeg in all one ounce and a half; the juice of three lemons and rind of two, a little salt, half a pint of brandy, a pint and a half of wine. The spices and liquor should be put in last. Three quarters of a pound of sugar sifted. Mix all together and press it hard into a glazed jar and cover with paper slipt in brandy. The jar also must be rinsed with brandy.

Sussex recipe c 1800. A later meatless version follows.

Mincemeat without meat

Quarter of a pound each of raisins, currants, sultanas, dried figs and chopped suet; half a pound each of chopped apples and sugar, two ounces of candied peel, half a teaspoon mixed spice, pinch of salt, the juice and rind of an orange and half a pint of rum. Mix thoroughly and put in jam jars until required.

Christmas Cake

Wash two pounds and a half of fresh butter in water first, and then in rose water. Beat the butter to a cream, beat twenty egg yolks and whites separately half an hour each, have ready two pounds and a half of the finest flour well dried and kept hot, likewise a pound and a half of sugar, pounded and sifted, one ounce of spice in finest powder, three pounds of currants nicely cleaned and dry, half a pound of almonds blanched, and three quarters of a pound of sweetmeats cut not too thin. Let all be kept by the fire, mix all the dry ingredients, pour the eggs strained to the butter, mix half a pint of sweet wine with a large glass of brandy, pour it to the butter and eggs, mix them well, then have all the dry things put in by degrees, beat them very thoroughly, you can hardly do it too much. Having half a pound of raisins chopped as fine as possible, mix them carefully so that there should be no lump, and add a tea cup full of orange flower water. Beat the ingredients together a full hour at least. Have a hoop well buttered, or if you have none, a tin or copper cake pan. Take a white paper, doubled and buttered, and put in the pan round the edge – if the cake batter fill it more than three parts, space should be allowed for rising. Bake in a quiet oven. It will require three hours.

Susannah Hooker's Cookery Book 1828

EASTER

Good Friday was the day for hot cross buns. It appears these were not made at home, but were bought from the bakers' boys who were on the streets early in the morning with their cry:

Hot cross buns! Hot cross buns!
One a penny, two for twopence, Hot cross buns.

To keep them safe while at sea, Sussex fishermen carried a bun in a tin box from one Good Friday to the next. They believed they could not drown as long as they carried a Good Friday bun with them. The landlubbers were as superstitious, and in many homes a bun was hung from a nail in the kitchen; should any of the family fall ill a piece of the bun was broken off, pounded, mixed with hot water and given as medicine. Mothers kept a bun from the first Good Friday after a child's birth in a cotton or paper bag. This was pinned up in the child's bedroom to keep whooping cough at bay.

It was usual to eat roast lamb on Easter Sunday, the reference being to the Passover, with the mint sauce supplying the 'bitter herbs' – followed by Sussex Pond Pudding (see page 29).

HARVEST HOME

Harvest time was a highlight of the rural year. After the crops had been cut by teams of men wielding sickles, after the sheaves were bound, the shocks built, the threshing done – and the fields gleaned by the village women – came the great day of the Harvest Home supper. This was the feast laid on by the farmer for his men and their families to celebrate the gathering of the harvest.

Usually the harvest supper took place in the barn where long tables, perhaps decorated with miniature sheaves of wheat, were set up. If the weather were fine the tables were arranged outside.

The hymn, *Come Ye Thankful People, Come*, was sung, then foaming tankards of ale were banged on the tables to welcome the arrival of the roast goose, or roast beef, served with Sussex Drip Pudding and followed by generous helpings of fruity plum pudding, pumpkin pie and apple turnovers. After supper there were songs, speeches and story telling .

Pumpkin Pie

Fill a pie dish with diced pumpkin that has been boiled in a little water until tender, and diced cooking apples. Add some washed currants, a liberal helping of moist brown sugar, a big pinch of mixed spice and ground ginger. Souse well with lemon juice. Top with good short pastry and bake in a moderate to slow oven for about 40 minutes. Lift the lid and pour in three or four tablespoonfuls of thick rich cream, and serve at once.

Mary Ann Floate,Washington, c 1822

Brown George

These were very large apple turnovers baked especially for Harvest Home. They could be as big as 16 inches long and 12 inches wide. To make, fill rough puff pastry with peeled, cored and sliced apples, generous knobs of butter and plenty of brown sugar. Seal and crimp turnovers, wash with a milk and egg glaze, sprinkle with sugar and bake to a crisp, golden brown.

Harvest Pumpkin Custards

Boil one pound of diced pumpkin to a pulp with a little water and sugar. When cold beat in a knob of butter, a pinch of ground ginger, a pinch of cinnamon, two well beaten eggs and a pint of milk. Continue to beat for two or three minutes. Line a pie plate with puff pastry. Bake for a few minutes to set the pastry. Fill three parts with the pumpkin mixture and bake in a moderate oven for about 35 minutes.

Warden Pie

This used to be made with hard, long-keeping warden pears. Peel, quarter and simmer the pears in sweetened water for about two hours. Leave them to get cold. Line the edge of a pie dish with thin pastry. Fill the dish with the pears, add a little lemon juice and a wineglasss of claret or port. Top with pastry and bake. When serving, lift the lid and spoon in two or three tablespoons of rich thick cream.

Seed Cake

Rub six ounces of beef dripping into one and a half pounds of self raising flour. Add a pinch of salt, a teaspoon of caraway seeds, a little chopped candied peel, a pinch of nutmeg and sugar to taste. Whisk the whites of two eggs and beat the yolks. Stir these slowly into the dry ingredients with enough milk to make a soft dough, then beat well. Turn the mixture into a well greased tin and bake in a moderate oven for about one and a half hours.

Harvest Supper Puddings

Six pounds flour, seven pounds raisins, five pounds suet, one and a half pounds moist sugar, twelve eggs, two nutmegs, a little salt, a glass of rum, some raisin wine and a little milk if required to make it of proper consistency. Mix the ingredients together and separate into six puddings. Boil each for three and a half hours.

SOMETHING SAVOURY

A Sussex Sausage Roll

Rub two ounces of lard and a teaspoon of salt into two pounds of white flour and one pound wholemeal flour. Put two teaspoons of castor sugar and half an ounce of yeast in a small basin with a teacup of tepid milk and water and let this stand until the yeast has dissolved. Make a hole in the flour and pour in the yeast mixture. Have ready six pork sausages or one pound of sausage meat. Add tepid water to the flour and yeast, and work all together into a stiff dough. Knead well. Cut two or three holes in the top of the dough, cover with a warm cloth and put in a warm place to rise for one or more hours. Then cut off pieces of the dough, roll out to three quarters of an inch thick and enclose one whole pork sausage, or an equal amount of sausage meat, in each piece. Put the rolls on a baking sheet and stand in a warm place for fifteen minutes. Cook in a moderately quick oven for fifteen minutes then reduce the heat for a further thirty minutes, or until well baked. The fat from the sausages will be absorbed by the dough.

Old Sussex Potato and Cheese Cakes

Mix together half a pound of potatoes mashed with butter and salt, two ounces of flour, two ounces of strong, grated cheese and one beaten egg. Flatten pieces of the mixture between damp palms, place on a greased baking sheet and bake in the oven or on a griddle for about twelve minutes.

This is an old but still useful recipe. The cakes make an interesting addition to a cold buffet and, when big enough, are handy, edible food holders at barbecues.

To Fricassee Eggs

Boil eggs hard, take out some of the yolks whole: then cut the rest in quarters, yolks and white together. Set on some gravy with a little shred thyme and parsley in it, and when it boils up, put in your eggs, with a little grated nutmeg, and shake them up with a piece of butter till it is of a proper thickness. Serve it up hot.

Susannah Stacey

Shrimp Toast

Mix the yolks of two eggs, one small teaspoon of anchovy sauce and one teaspoon of milk in a small pan and heat it gently until a sauce forms. Add half a pint of shrimps, stir until warmed and serve on hot buttered toast.

Ramekins

Put some Parmesan cheese into a stewpan, bruise it with a quarter of a pound of fresh butter, a gill of water, salt, and an anchovy cut small; boil them together, and put in as much flour as the sauce will take up; keep it over the fire till it is in a thick paste, and then put it into a stewpan with the yolks of twelve eggs. Beat up the whites quite stiff till they will bear an egg, then mix with the rest. Drop them into square paper cases. If well made they will be light, and of a fine colour.

Susannah Stacey

Roasted Cheese for After Dinner

Grate three ounces of good cheese, mix it with the yolks of two eggs, four ounces of grated bread, and three ounces of butter; beat the whole in a mortar, with a dessert-spoonful of mustard, some salt and pepper. Toast some bread, cut it into proper pieces, lay the paste as above thick upon them, put them into a Dutch oven, covered with a dish, till hot through; remove the dish and let the cheese just brown. Serve as hot as possible.

Susannah Stacey

Eggs with Onions and Mushrooms

When the eggs are boiled hard, take out the yolks entire, and cut the whites in slips, with some onions and mushrooms. Fry the onions and mushrooms, throw in the whites and turn about a little. Pour off the fat, if there be any; flour the onions, etc., and put to them a little good gravy. Boil this up, then put in the yolks, and add a little pepper and salt. Let the whole simmer for about a minute. Serve it up.

Susannah Stacey

Curious Manner of Making Eggs Larger Than That of an Ostrich

Part the yolks from the whites of a number of common eggs, and strain them into two different pans or basins, according to the size and quantity wanted. To make a large egg, take a bladder and fill in as much yolk as will be, when tied up round like a ball and boiled, of the magnitude wanted; and, having boiled it hard, put it into another bladder surrounded with sufficient white, tie it up in an oval form, and boil that also hard. A very large egg thus prepared has a very fine effect with a grand salad; and, in ragouts, etc., one large yolk alone, which may easily be made, looks extremely pleasing.

Susannah Stacey

Golden Eggs

Hard boil four eggs, chill and shell them and cut into small dice. Lightly fry half a Spanish onion in three ounces of butter. Sprinkle into the onion when tender a dessertspoon of dry mustard, mix in the eggs and stir briskly over the fire until nicely browned. Have ready four squares of well buttered toast, very hot, dish the mixture on these and eat at once.

Lady Gage

Eggs Fried in Paste

Boil six eggs for three minutes, put them into cold water, take off the shells (but do not break the whites), wrap the eggs in the trimmings of puff paste: brush them over with egg, and sprinkle a few breadcrunbs over them; have lard or clarified butter in a stewpan, sufficient for the eggs to swim when they are put in; when the lard is hot put the eggs in, and fry them a nice gold colour; when done, lay them on a napkin.

Susannah Stacey

PICKLES AND PRESERVES

F EW sights are more satisfying to the cook than a larder or cupboard stacked with jewel-bright jars of jams and jellies, pickles and chutneys – all home made. It was always the case and is more so today when such a diverse range of preserves is available in the stores. Some of these are excellent, but some are tasteless, of peculiar consistency and dubious colour. To embark upon preserving may seem daunting to the novice, but in truth it is very simple, as are the utensils needed – a stainless steel or enamel pan, a jelly bag, a wooden spoon and some jars.

Pickled Grapes

Unripe grapes are best. Make some sweet spiced white vinegar, using demerara sugar, pour it over the washed and dried grapes and let it stand for 24 hours. Bring to the boil very gently, bottle and seal. Serve with cold game or poultry, ham and tongue.

Mock Capers

Collect the seed heads from nasturtiums and drop them into small bottles of white vinegar and a little salt.

Pickled Green Figs

Fully grown but unripe figs left at the end of the season can be preserved in syrup. Steep 6lb figs (cut with a small cross at the base) in lime water (one gallon water, two teacups slaked lime) for 24 hours. Rinse the fruit several times and dry them. Make a syrup with 6lb sugar and 6pt water and when it is boiling add the figs. Boil until the figs are transparent (three to four hours). Half way through the cooking add two lemon slices, and half an hour before the end add slices of preserved ginger. Pack the figs into wide necked jars and seal.

Pickled Walnuts

Boil some salt and water and throw over the walnuts and leave to soak for two or three days. Then put the walnuts in a large jar and pour boiling vinegar over them, putting in a little sliced ginger, onion and some whole peppercorns.

Mrs Gould 1818

Pickled Crab Apples

To every gallon of white vinegar add one ounce of common salt, one ounce of mustard seed, half an ounce of mace, half an ounce of whole pepper, half an ounce of cloves, two capsicums or one dr of cayenne, and two bay leaves. Boil for 20 minutes and when cool pour over the crab apples - having previously washed them in common salt water – and let dry before putting into jars.

Miss Kennard, Hamsey 1896

Pickled Samphire

Lay green samphire in a pan, and throw two handfuls of salt over it; cover with spring water, and let it lie twenty-four hours, then put it into a saucepan, throw in a handful of salt and cover with good vinegar. Cover close, and set it over a slow fire. Take if off the moment it is green and crisp, for should it remain till soft it will be spoiled. Put it in the pickling pot, and cover it close. When cold, tie it down with a bladder and leather, and keep it for use; or it will keep all the year in a strong brine of salt and water. Throw it into vinegar just before being used.

Susannah Stacey

To Pickel Young Hartichoaks

Take a quantity of young hartichoaks & lay them in salt water 24 hours, strain them & boyle them tender as for eating, then pull of ye outside leaves untill they look like Acorn then make a pickle of vinegar. Boyle two quarts & pour upon an ounce of white peper, a few cloves, four or five blades of mace & one nuttmeg sliced. Let your pickell stand close covered untill it is cold, and pour it upon your hartichoaks. Keep them close covered & in a fortnight you may begin to eat them.

Arundel ms

Spiced Plums

Boil three pints of malt vinegar with three pounds of demerara sugar, three inches of cinnamon stick, one ounce of cloves, one ounce of peppercorns for ten minutes. Add three quarts of plums and simmer very carefully for another two minutes. Care must be taken not to let it get mushy or the final appearance of the pickle will be spoiled. Plums must be inserted into the jars very carefully and covered when cold. Cherries, gooseberries, currants, figs and damsons can also be pickled in this way, although simmering time must be adjusted to suit.

Pickled Onions

Peel shallots, wipe them with a clean damp cloth and place in glass jars. Add one dessertspoon of demerara sugar to each before they are filled with cold (not boiled) vinegar. Boil a handful of pickling spice in another pint of vinegar and leave it until cold. Then add it to the jars with a little spice. Seal the jars and place them in a cool place for three months before using.

To Pickle Red Cabbage

Cut ye cabbidge as thin as you can, lay it in a pott in thick rows, between every row throw a Little salt & beaten Pepper when yr pot is full pour in yr vinegar cold and be sure to thrust ye cabbidge down in ye pott as close as possible then tye it down close. Twill keep good a great while.

Arundel ms

To Pickle Cowcumbers

Take your Cowcumbers and just wash them in Salt and water, and lay them to drain, then lay a layer of Cowcumbers, then lay some dill-seed, Cloves, Mace and whole pepper, so laying them to ye top. Then take Vinegar and Boyl it, and when it boils pour it into them and cover them close up, and let them stand a fortnight then boyl up your Vinegar again, and keep them very close.

Phildelphia Shoebridge

Sloe and Blackberry Cheese

Take equal quantities of sloes and blackberries and put them in a preserving pan with a pound of sugar to every pound of fruit. Bring to the boil and boil fast for about 45 minutes. Skim, then crush the fruit through a sieve and pot up.

Bullace Cheese

Put full ripe Bullace (wild damsons) into a pot and to every quart of them put a quarter of a pound of loaf sugar beaten fine. Bake them in a moderately heated oven till soft, and rub them through a hair sieve. To every pound of pulp add half a pound of loaf sugar beaten fine then boil it an hour and a half over a slow fire and keep stirring all the time. Then pour it into pots, tie brandy paper over and keep them in a cool place; when it has stood a few months it will cut very bright and fine.

Mary Bays 1803

Damson Cheese

Gather the fruit in September or October, the later the better. The damsons must be perfectly dry and if possible gathered warm in the sunshine. Bake the fruit in a stone jar, and to every four pound of fruit weigh one pound of sugar. Put the fruit over the fire again in a pan, let it boil quickly till it begins to look dry; take out the stones, crack them, and put the kernels to the damsons. Add the sugar, stirring it well in, and simmer for two hours slowly; then boil it quickly for about half an hour or until the sides of the pan commence to candy; then pour into glass jars or pots.

Edward Shoosmith 1937

Apple Cheese

Take any kinds of apples; quarter them, core and peel. Be sure and cut out any bruised parts and wipe them. Stew to a pulp; then take a coarse jelly bag or cloth, fastening each corner to a strong kitchen chair with a basin underneath. When cooked and cooled scoop some into the jelly bag and squeeze very hard until nothing remains but refuse. Put three quarters of a pound of sugar to a pint of apple juice and pulp and boil till stiff. Pour into jars with a little spirit on the top. This will keep for years. Siberian crabs are sometimes used instead of apples and are good but require more sugar. Some people add cloves, cinnamon or a pinch of ginger to the pulp.

Old Sussex recipe book

Orange Marmalett

Take two pounds of Oranges and pare them, & pick out ye meat and boyle ye white Peels in several waters till ye Bitterness be out. Dry them in a cloth, cut them in thinn peices, boyle a pint of Pipen Jelly, put your meat of ye orang & a pound of Loafe sugar, then let it boyle halfe an hour, then put your Peel in. Have ready another pound of Sugar beaten which must strow in at times as it boyls, an let it boyle till it Jelly.

Arundel ms

Candy Pipens

Take fair large yellow pipens (apples) pare them & bore a hole thro them & lay them in a broad earthen dish & set them into an Oven & strow fine sugar on them. Sprinkle a little Rose or Orange flower water on that sugar then bake them in an oven as hott as for manchet & stop ye oven, so let them stand half an hour, then take them out & lay them on a Lattice of wire or Basket makers rods. So let them be dryed three or four days & then they will look as clear as amber & be finely canded.

Arundel ms

Lemon Cheese

Grate the rind of three lemons and strain the juice. Mix with ten and a half ounces of sugar and three beaten eggs, in a stone jar. Place the jar in a saucepan of boiling water and add two ounces of butter cut into small pieces. Leave the jar in the boiling water for two hours, stirring occasionally and never allowing the mixture to boil. Pour into jars and cover as for jam. Lemon cheese made this way will keep about two months.
Sussex farmhouse recipe c 1930

Apple Ginger Preserve

Take four pounds of sugar, four pounds of hard apples, three pints of water and two dessert spoons of ginger essence. Boil the sugar in the water to a rich syrup, then add the ginger essence. Pare, core and cut up the apples. Put them into cold water to prevent their turning brown, then place them in the syrup and boil until transparent, taking care not to let them break. Place in warmed preserving jars, pour the syrup over and seal while hot.

Apple Marmalade

Cut three pounds of peeled and cored apples into small pieces and put in a pan with a pint of water, two ounces of fine shredded candied peel and the grated rind and juice of one lemon. Simmer until soft then add four pounds of sugar, stirring until it dissolves. Continue to simmer until the marmalade thickens, then pot up in warmed jars.

Quince Marmalade

Pare your quinces, cut them in quarters and core them and throw them into water as you pare them (to prevent discolouration). Then weigh them, and allow half a pint of water to one pound of quinces, add half a pint of water. The cores with the seeds must be kept in a bit of muslin and let it lay in the pan with the quinces. Cover very close so that no steam escapes and stew gently, looking at it once an hour and then stir it for fear of burning and when you see the quinces are very tender and begin to look red, take out the cores and break your quinces very small. Then stew it again till it is thick and will jelly. *English Folk Cookery Association, Sussex Branch, 1936*

To Make White Marmelet Mrs Harris' Way

Take to a pound of quinces tenderly parboyled a pound of double refined sugar and halfe a pint of faire water. Keep out half of the sugar and put in as it boyles. Let it boyle quick and keep sturring all the while. When you see tis enough, which it will in a little time, put it up in glasses.

Ann Lord

To Preserve Mulberries Whole

Set some mulberries over the fire in a preserving pan; draw from them a pint of juice; when it is strained, take three pounds of sugar beaten fine, wet the sugar with the pint of juice, boil and skim it, put in two pounds of ripe mulberries, and let them stand in the syrup till they are thoroughly warm; set them on the fire, and boil them gently; do them half enough and put them by in the syrup till next day; boil them gently again, till the syrup is pretty thick, and will stand in round drops; when cold put them into pots for use.

Lucy Young, Steyning (1781-1852)

Brandy Cherries

Cut half the stem from each cherry, washing them in brandy, put them into a large wide mouthed bottle. Fill it with the cherries and then pour over them as much brandy as the bottle will hold. Sweeten it with white sugar candy finely powdered, a pound to two quarts of brandy. The bottle will want filling up several times.

Mrs Gould 1818

Candied Primroses or Cowslips

Gather primroses or cowslips when dry and pull the flowers from the green calyx. Make a syrup of sugar and water and boil it until when a little dropped into cold water is crisp. Then put in the flowers for a minute. Take them out and dry them on a sieve. Leave them in a warm place to dry and sprinkle them with finely powdered sugar. Gently open the flowers and sift any superfluous sugar from them. Keep them in a dry place.

Seventeenth century Sussex ms

To Candy Rosemary Flowres

Take the weight of yoe flowres in sugar and put them in a pewter dish over a soft fire styrring them about till they begin to crumble. They are very good for the headache.

Ann Lord

Elderflower Vinegar

Put two gallons of strong ale alegar (sour ale or malt vinegar) to a peck of the pips of elder flowers. Set it in the sun in a stone jar for a fortnight, and then filter it through a flannel bag. When it is drawn off put it into small bottles, in which it will preserve its flavour better than in large ones. In mixing the flowers and alegar together, be careful not to drop any of the stalks among the pips.

Mary Bays 1805

Gooseberry or Currant Vinegar

Procure a quantity of either of the above sorts of fruit, or a portion of each when nearly ripe, and bruise them to a pulp, and to every gallon of fruit put two gallons and a half of boiling water; let it stand three days, stirring it occasionally; strain it through a sieve, measure the quantity to be put in the cask, and to every gallon add two pounds of coarse sugar dissolved in boiling water, which will be sufficient to give a fulness of flavour. Let the whole stand till it be milk warm, then add a portion of new yeast, when it will soon ferment; after which add a few handsful of the spent fruit to every two gallons, and let it stand in a warm place, which will soon complete the proper acidity and render it an admired vinegar.

Richard Shoosmith, Brighthelmston 1826

Raisin Vinegar

Take forty pounds of common Malaga or Lexia rasins, bruise them well with the stalks, and add sufficient water to cover them, until the liquor be well fermented, then fill up the hogshead with either new or old cider; stir it well and place it in a warm situation, and when fine, it may be drawn from the cask.

Richard Shoosmith, Brighthelmston 1826

Verjuice

Verjuice, used in sauces and in place of lemon juice in old recipes, was made with crab apples when the kernels had turned black. Pick over the crab apples, removing stalks and any bruised parts; pile them in a heap to sweat and then squeeze them through a hair bag. Put the juice in bottles and stop them for use.

BEES AND HONEY

A swarm of bees in May is worth a load of hay;
A swarm of bees in June is worth a silver spoon;
A swarm of bees in July is not worth a butterfly;
Old Sussex rhyme

THE nectar rich plants of the Downs, of the fertile Weald and the western coastal plain once gave Sussex its own distinctive varieties of honey. So valued was this honey, with its scent and taste of clovers, sainfoin, medick, charlock, bramble berries and herb willow that a commercial apiary was set up at East Dean in the 1920s. There were hundreds of hives over the hills, and in the old quarries, in which family groups of bees of a distinct type were kept together.

Until the last quarter of the nineteenth century almost every cottage garden had its row of straw bee hives, called skeps, protected in winter by a cover of straw called a hackle.

There was an art to making the skeps. Clean straw was used, bound with pliant bramble or cane. The early skeps were of a simple dome shape. A greatly improved design was the two tier hive which had a lower half with a flat roof with a hole in it giving access to the smaller hive on top. The hackle was a pyramid of neat straw rope from which hung a long thick fringe of wheat straw, not quite touching the ground, providing excellent protection in rough weather.

When the time came to take the honey from the skep, the industrious workers used to be sacrificed. The cottagers and farmers knew of no other way to harvest their life's work.

Country people had an intimate relationship with bees. If a bee settled on a living bough of a tree all would be well with the family, but if on a piece of dead wood, then death would occur. Bees were notified of births, marriages and deaths – called telling the bees. If this were not done then the bees would die or fly away. The teller would go to the hive and knock three times with a door key, chanting 'the master is dead', or 'a child has been born'.

Before sugar became available honey was the only means of sweetening. It was almost as good as money. The seventh century King Ina of Sussex is said to have imposed a rent of dolias of honey. A dolia was a large case shaped jar for storing liquids.

As well as sweetening, honey was invaluable for medicinal purposes and for making mead and metheglin. Honey and glycerine, sometimes with a scraping of nutmeg, was taken for coughs and colds, it was beaten up with salt and raw egg to anoint sprains, spread hot on linen to treat boils. A traditional cure for whooping cough was to place a new laid egg (in its shell) in vinegar until it dissolved, stir in some honey and dose the patient three times a day.

Hum, a tonic, was made from the washings of the combs seasoned with pepper. To make honey tea, a tonic for tiredness, indigestion and dyspepsia, dissolve one tablespoon of honey in a cup of freshly boiled water and sip it as hot as possible.

Mead, a sparkling golden drink made with new honey, was brewed in the monasteries. The monks drank it themselves and sold the surplus to bring in money. True mead was made only from honey, water and yeast, but the medieval recipe degenerated over the centuries and more ingredients were added. Metheglin is a more delicate brew made with fine honey and flavoured with fragrant herbs.

Metheglin

To 13 gallons of water put 30lb of honey, boil and scum it well. Take rosemary, thyme, bay leaves and sweet briar, one handful of each, boil it an hour. Put it in a tub with a little ground malt and stir till it is lukewarm. Put in yeast spread on a toast. When the liquor is covered over with the yeast put it up in a barrel. Take of cloves, mace and nutmegs one and a half ounces, of ginger sliced one ounce. Bruise the spice, tie it up in a muslin and hang it in the vessel, stopping it up close for use.

Strong Mead

Take eighteen gallons of water, make it scalding hot, then put in sixty four pounds of Honey, take eight ounces of hoppes Sew them up with a stone to sink them. Keep it boyling for an hour & scuming it all ye while, & when it is thus boyled, work it with Yest as you doe ale & turn it up & when dun working bung it downe. Lett it stand 3 months & then bottle it off.

Arundel ms

White Small Meade

Take ten Quarts of Spring water, when it is ready to boyle, put into it two pints of Honey & one pound of Loafe Sugar beaten, then boyle & scum it as long as any rise, then take it off ye fire. Put in three Lemons peels & juice, cut them as for a Coole Tankard of wine when tis could, put in two cloves, 4 spoonfulls of yest, & put it in an Earthen pott, in two or three days you may Bottle it & it will be fitt to drink in a week or tenn days.

Arundel ms

Sussex Mead

Bring 8 quarts of water and 6lb honey slowly to the boil, add cinnamon, ginger, mace, or cloves, as fancy suggests. Simmer gently until reduced to 3 quarts. Pour into an earthenware pan and when cool add half a pint of yeast. Keep at 75 deg for three days. Pour into a cask. Close the bung when fermentation subsides. Keep at least twelve months.

Mead Champagne

Take 1lb honey and comb to the quart of water (comb honey is not absolutely essential but it is considered better to use it); add a few cloves, two or three per quart; heat up till all is dissolved, allow to cool; the wax will come to the top and set, when it is taken off. Strain into a crock or other fairly open vessel, float a small piece of toast on it and place a little yeast on the toast; leave in a warm place for a week or so. Bottle, leaving stoppers loose; when all hissing has finished, screw down tight. Leave at least six months before drinking.

BEERS, WINES, CUPS AND CORDIALS

THREE centuries into their occupation of Britain the Romans, who until then had imported their wines, were finally permitted by the Emperor Probus to cultivate vines and make wine here.

They established vineyards at Cissbury, Buxted and Battle but when the legions left in 407 most of them fell into neglect. Yet the vines survived and the next invaders, the Saxons, inherited a species producing tiny sweet green grapes. More than 1,000 years later, in smuggling days, when a keg of brandy was left for those who turned their backs 'as the gentlemen went by', bunches of these little green grapes, and sugar candy, were added to the keg and fastened down with pig bladder until Christmas.

With the vineyards derelict the Saxons resorted to ale and mead. Ale was the traditional brew until the fourteenth century when hops, in use in the Low Countries to give beer a bite, were introduced into Kent and East Sussex. Hops give beer its distinctive bitter flavour and also act as a preservative, enabling it to be kept in good condition for much longer than unhopped ale.

The south east corner of England became the centre of the hop growing industry. Hop gardens were established and oasthouses built to dry the harvest.

Picking the hops from the bines was a labour intensive business and at harvest time travelling people, women from the coastal towns and villagers made their way to the hop gardens both to earn a few shillings and enjoy an annual 'holiday' in the countryside. Rudimentary huts were provided for the pickers at some gardens and other owners allocated a barn or outhouse. At the end of the season there was the hop pickers' supper to look forward to.

Britain's entry into the European Community brought an end to the Hops Marketing Board and rules were introduced banning the growing of seeded hops. Only the better hop soils in Kent, Hertfordshire and Worcestershire are able to produce the finer unseeded varieties successfully and economically.

In earlier days landowners considered it a duty to brew good honest beer for their workforce, especially as much of the liquor sold in inns was adulterated. After the first brew of fine beer, small beer (swanky), usually drunk by the labourers for breakfast, was brewed. Compared with today's beers this, too, was strong, but was regarded scornfully by the men, who said there was no need to pen it in hurdles as it was too weak to run away.

When they reported for work early in the morning the farm workers found small iron bound oak kegs waiting for them, with leather thongs to slip on to the hames of the horses' collars. Each took about a quart of beer to the fields.

The ingredients of the beer were pure rain water, malt and hops. At Susannah Stacey's Stantons Farm, East Chiltington, two bushels of malt and a pound and a half of hops made eighteen gallons of good ale, eighteen gallons of table beer and nine gallons of small beer. Sometimes a hogshead of porter would be made. To two bushels and a half of highly coloured malt, there would be added 'three pounds of hops, two pounds and a half of treacle, four pounds of colouring, two pounds and a half of liquorice root, one ounce of Spanish liquorice, and of salt, salts of tartar, alum, capsicum and ginger, of each a small quantity'. The malt was mashed and the hops boiled as in the beer brewing.

For centuries country people made wine from cowslips and marigolds, coltsfoot and dandelion, primroses and elderflower, raspberries and currants. The green gooseberry wine of Sussex was, it was claimed, better than champagne. The still room was an important adjunct to every country house. Here wines and cordials were made, spirits distilled, and balm water, rosemary water, syrup of roses or violets and citron water concocted.

WINES

Elderberry Wine

Gather the elderberries ripe and dry, pick them and bruise them with your hands and strain them. Set the liquor by in glazed earthen vessels for twelve hours to settle. Put to every pint of juice a pint and a half of water and to every gallon of this liquor three pounds of Lisbon sugar; set in a kettle over the fire, and when it is ready to boil, clarify it with the whites of four or five eggs; let it boil an hour and when it is almost cold, work it with strong ale yeast and tun it, filling up the vessel from time to time with the same liquor, saved on purpose, as it sinks by working. In a month's time if the vessel holds about eight gallons, it will be fine and fit to bottle and after bottling will be fit to drink in two months; but if the vessel be larger it must stand longer in proportion, three to four months at least for a hogshead. Note: All liquors must be fined before they are bottled or else they will grow sharp and ferment in the bottle. Add to every gallon of this liquor a pint of strong mountain wine, but not such as has the borachio or hog's skin flavour. This wine will be very good and pleasant and keep good for several years.

Barbara Young, Steyning, c1790

Gooseberry Wine

Gather your gooseberries in a dry season when they are half-ripe, pick them and bruise them in a tub with a wooden mallet, for no metal is proper; take about the quantity of a peck of the gooseberries; put them in a cloth made of horse-hair, and press them as much as possible without breaking the seeds; repeat this till all your gooseberries are bruised, adding to this pressed juice the other in the tub; and to every gallon three pounds of powder sugar; stir it together till all the sugar is dissolved and then put it in a vessel, which must be quite filled with it. If the vessel holds about ten or twelve gallons it must stand a fortnight or three weeks; or if about twenty gallons about four or five weeks to settle in a cool place. Draw off the wine from the lees. After you have discharged the lees from the vessel, return the clear liquor into the vessel again and let it stand three months, if the cask is about three gallons, or between four and five months if it be twenty gallons, and then bottle it. This wine, if truly prepared according to the above directions, will improve every year.

Mountain Wine

Pick out the stalks of Malaga raisins, chop them small and put five pounds to every gallon of cold spring water; let them steep a fortnight or more, then squeeze out the liquor and barrel it in a vessel fit for it; fume the vessel with brimstone. Do not stop it close till the hissing is over. Put half a pint of French brandy to every gallon of wine.

Betony Wine

Press as much wood betony as possible into a large boiler. Cover with water and boil for one hour. When cold strain into a vessel and add three pounds of sugar to each gallon of liquor. When it has done working, cork down, adding a little sugar candy to fine it. Not to be drunk under six months.

Raison Wine

Take four pound of Raisons of ye Sun pick them, cleane & stone them & put them in an Earthern pott; then take 4 Gallons of faire water & let it boyle half an hour. When it is boyled pour it into ye pott to ye Raisons & put to it two pound of sugar & 4 Lemons squeased in, & ye peel of 2 of them or all of them if you like it. Stirr them together & cover ye pott very close till next day, then put in your hand to

Wood betony   squeese yr Raisons & Cover ye pott againe till next day, then strain it out & put it through a jelly bagg & bottle it, but fill not yr Bottles two full, tye down ye Corks & in 8 or 10 days twill be fitt to drink.
Arundel ms

Wine of Currants, Goosberries & Rasberries

Gather your fruit full ripe, pick & bruise them in a marble morter, & to every gallon of Pulp, put two Gallons of Water, after it has been boild & stood to be cold, let it stand in a Tub 24 hours to ferment, then run it thro a Hair Sieve, but let no hand touch it, let it have its time to run. To every gallon of this liquor put four pound of pretty good sugar, stir it well & put it into your Vessell, let it stand till fine then Bottle it. As ye Rasberries are ripe sooner than ye other fruit you must make a syrup of them & add it to ye other juice.
Arundel ms

Elderflower Wine

Boil eighteen pounds of white powdered sugar in six gallons of water, and two whites of eggs well beaten; skim it, and put in a quarter of a peck of elderflowers from the tree that bears white berries; do not keep them on the fire. When cool, stir it, and put in six spoonfuls of lemon-juice, four or five of yeast, and beat it well into the liquor, stir it well every day; put six pounds of the best raisins, stoned, into the cask, and tun the wine. Stop it close, and bottle in six months. When well kept this wine will pass very well for Frontiniac.

Susannah Stacey

Elderflower Champagne

Place two big flower heads in a large basin with two tablespoons of white vinegar, the juice of one lemon and the rind cut into four, one gallon of cold water and one and a half pounds of loaf sugar. Leave for twenty four hours, strain into screw top bottles and put aside for three months.

Coltsfoot Wine

Pour twelve gallons of boiling water over five gallons of coltsfoot flowers; let it stand till cold, then strain it off; add three pounds of raw sugar to a gallon; boil it till clear. When nearly cold put in the peel of twelve lemons and of as many oranges with a few spoonfuls of yeast. Let it stand a little time to work. Then put it into the cask with the juice of the oranges and lemons. Let it stand six months, then bottle.

Susannah Stacey

Burnet Wine

Pour one gallon of boiling water on one gallon of burnet flowers; let it stand twenty-four hours; then strain it and squeeze the flowers well. Then boil the liquor with three and half pounds of loaf sugar to each gallon. Work it and put it into the barrel with half a pound of raisins chopped to each gallon. Let it stand twelve months and bottle.

Susannah Stacey

Quince Wine

Take ripe quinces and wipe off the fur very carefully; take out the cores, bruise them as you would apples for cyder, and press out the juice; to every gallon of which add two pounds and a half of loaf sugar. Stir it together till the sugar is dissolved; afterwards put it into your cask; and when it has done fermenting, bung it up well. Let it stand till March before you bottle it. This will improve by being kept two or three years.

Susannah Stacey

Woodruff Wine

Put a pint of white wine and two of red into a jug with sufficient sugar to sweeten it. Cut an orange, without peeling it, into thick slices and add it to the wine; then throw into it some bunches of woodruff well washed and drained. Cover the jug and leave it till the next day.

Hogasses Wine

Gather hawthorn berries when ripe, clean them and put them in a glazed crock or pan. Pour boiling water over them, one pint to a pound of berries. Let it stand for six weeks. Skim off the crust and strain the liquid through cloth. Add one pound of sugar to one pound of fruit and let it stand in a jar, which must be full. Keep a little of the liquid aside to fill up the jar from time to time so that it may 'work'. When working ceases bottle the wine and let it stand as long as possible before drinking.

A Cooling Wine Usually Drunke
at Summer Entertainments

Take a pound of reasons of the sunn and slitt them, a pound of loafe sugar, to great leamons or three leasser ones, cut in sliciss; put all these in an earthen creame pott, then take to gallons of water and boyle it half an hour and put it to the ingrediance boyling hott. Then lett it stand three days close covered, then strain it and lett it stand three hours and then bottell it up and stop it close: keep it coole: in a fortnight it will be ripe and it will last drinking a fortnight. If you please you may put the juce of two or three leamons in ye ingrediances.

Ann Lord

Dandelion Wine

Cover the heads with boiling water, leave them for a day or two, and then add the rind of a lemon and an orange and a pound of lump sugar and a pinch of ground ginger to every quart of liquid and boil it. Then strain it into a crock, put a bit of yeast in it, and leave it for three or four days, strain and bottle.

Marigold Wine

Boil one gallon of water and two pounds of sugar for an hour and add one and a half ounces of syrup of citron. When lukewarm put on it a toast spread with yeast to work two days. Then put in a peck of marigold flowers and two lemons sliced with the rinds to each gallon of liquid. Add brandy or some white or Rhenish wine, one pint to each gallon. Then tun it up.

Charles Carter, 1732

CORDIALS

Sussex pottery
spirit flask and
wine bottle

Cherry brandy

Take a glass bottle that holds six quarts, put in it four quarts of good ffrench Brandy, three pound of good sugar, about 30 or 40 cloves, two nutmegs cut in quarters, half an ounce of Cinamon bruised & broke about an inch long, four pound of good ripe Cherrys Red. Pull of ye stalkes, then put in ye Cherrys without taking out ye stones & put them in ye bottle, then put two or three candid orang (peel) cut into square pieces. Cork up ye bottle, put it in ye sun two months, let it be shaken once a day, tis an admirable Cordial.

Arundel ms

Sloe Gin

Fill a screw-topped fruit bottle with sloes that have been de-stalked and wiped clean. Add about quarter of a pound or more of sugar candy and fill up the bottle with gin. Shake the bottle twice daily for a month, strain and bottle. Keep as long as possible before drinking.

Garibaldi Liqueur

Put one gallon of gin in a two gallon stone bottle; add one gallon of sloes, two pounds of loaf sugar, one pound of sugar candy, half an ounce of bitter almonds, peeled and bruised. Let it be shaken often. This may remain three months before bottling, when it must be strained.

Garibaldi, the Italian statesman, was a guest at Stantons Farm, East Chiltington, in 1865. He had been given an introduction from Susannah Stacey's nephew, William Stanford, who lived in Naples where he worked at the Bank of Italy. In Garibaldi's honour Mrs Stacey created this special liqueur – plum coloured to match his coat.

105

Arthur Beckett, publisher, author and founder of the Sussex County Magazine, was walking with his wife near Heathfield and-called at a cottage for a glass of water. They were invited in and each was given a wine glass of a pale yellow coloured fluid.

'What is it?' they asked.

'Oh, be joyful' the woman answered.

So taken were the Becketts with the delicious nectar that they begged the recipe.

Oh, Be Joyful

Now take of loaf-sugar three pounds of the best. Of sixteen Seville oranges the rind, paring it as thin as your skill may allow you. Of Saffron take three penny-worth, if your dealer is an honest man: if you know him for his parsimony you will take fourpenny worth; if for his generosity in his dealings take two penny-worth only. Of gin you will take one gallon of the best. Now you must proceed in the making of this cordial with due ceremony, for in the making of cordials and home-brewed wines ceremony is not to be set aside if you wish for the full pleasure that comes from these simple delights. Therefore, you will take, in the first place, a stone jar. Let it be worthy of the honour you do it, wide of mouth and deep in the belly. And being assured that it is soiled by no speck of dirt or dust, you must put therein your orange-rind, your loaf-sugar, and your saffron. Then, on to these you will pour your gin, and cover the mouth of the jar very carefully. Now you will set the jar in a cool cellar, of which you will carry the key for eight days, for you must not trust the curiosity of those about you. But you alone must visit your jar once at the end of each day for a great stirring and mixing with a wooden spoon. And if you are true to yourself you will refrain from tasting, for tasting spoils anticipation. But at the end of the time laid down, if you are free from care, you will take the bottles that contained your gin, and one over for the surplus, and, straining the liquid through fine linen, you will bottle the cordial; and see that your corks be good. Next, you may taste from the bottle containing the surplus, but no more, for to be in good condition your cordial should rest a year (for so much time is necessary for mellowness), the while you possess yourself in patience.

Dicker ware spirit flask

CIDER

Sussex was once famous for its cider, centuries before the West Country and Herefordshire took the honours. Cider is still produced in the county, most notably by Merrydown of Horam, but the once prolific local industry is extinct.

References to Sussex cider occur as early as 1275 when Richard de Clifford was accused of taking an apple mill and press from the widow of Geoffrey de Bassco in Pagham. The Nonae Rolls of 1341 listed eighty parishes were cider was made, seventy four in the west of the county, six in the east. At that time the church gained a substantial portion of its annual income from cider tithes.

Cider press

In February 1684 a patent was taken out by Richard Haines of Sullington for: 'An art or method of improving, preparing and meliorating cyder, so as to put the strength or goodness of two or three hogsheads of the liquor into one, and render the same much more wholesome and delightful'.

He described the process: 'Put one hogshead of cyder and some fruit juice into a copper still, and then put the same into your other hogshead and fill it up; stirr it about well and keep it close stopt, except one day in ten or twenty let it lie open five or six hours. Within three months this will be as strong as the best French wines and as pleasing, though different in taste. Additional spirit and more sugar to pleasure will make this cider like canary, and one pint of good spirit added to a gallon of cider will make it equal to Spanish wines.'

Petworth cider was especially valued but the industry seems to have died out in the 1820s. The 1841 census reveals that there was no longer any cider making on a commercial scale although it continued to be pressed on some farms, for domestic consumption only, until as recently as fifty years ago.

DRINKS FOR WINTER NIGHTS
Sussex Jackut

Add to a pint of table beer of ale a tablespoon of brandy, a teaspoon of brown sugar, a little grated nutmeg or ginger and a roll of very thin cut lemon peel.

Brown Betty

Dissolve a quarter of a pound of brown sugar in a pint of water, add a slice of lemon and let it stand for a quarter of an hour. Add a small quantity of cloves and cinnamon, half a pint of brandy and a quart of strong ale. Stir it well together and float on it two slices of toasted bread sprinkled with nutmeg and ginger.

Jump upon Betty

Grate half a nutmeg into a jug, to which put one bottle of sherry. Boil a quart of ale and pour into it. Be careful not to break the head of the ale in boiling.

Lambs' Wool

Mix the pulp of six large, roasted apples with some raw brown sugar, grated nutmeg and a pinch of ginger. Add a quart of warmed, strong ale, taste, and adjust sugar. Serve in a bowl with small sweet cakes floating in the liquid.

Wassail bowl

To half a pound of sugar in a bowl add a pint of warm beer, a grating of nutmeg, a pinch of ginger and four glasses of sherry. Then add five more pints of beer (cold). Stir and sweeten to taste. Cover the bowl and let it stand for two or three hours, after which put in three or four slices of thin toast, a few slices of lemon and lumps of loaf sugar rubbed on the peel of a lemon.

Toby's Punch

In a glass, dissolve three or four knobs of sugar with boiling water, add one wine glass of old rum, half a wine glass of port or sherry and half a wine glass of orange bitters. Fill the tumbler with boiling water and stir.

Mulled Ale

Put a pint of ale, a clove, a little whole ginger, a small knob of butter and a teaspoon of sugar into a saucepan and bring it to the boil. Meanwhile beat two eggs with a tablespoon of old ale and pour the boiling ale on to this mixture. Pass the mixture from one jug to another two or three times, return it to the saucepan and heat almost to boiling point.

Mulled Port

Boil a small quantity of cinnamon, cloves and mace in a gill of water. Pour a bottle of port wine into this and when it is almost boiling add two lemons, thinly sliced. Sweeten to taste.

Mum

Take 32 gallons of water, boil it till a third part is wasted and brew it  according to Art with three and a half bushels of Malt, half a bushel of Ground Beans, and half a bushel of Oatmeal. Put the result of the brew into your cask and do not fill it too full and when it begins to work, put in a pound and a half of the inner rind of Fir or half a pound of tops of Fir and Birch instead of the inner rind. Our English Mum-makers use Sasseferas and ginger, the rind of walnut tree, Elecampane root, water cresses, and Horse Radish root rasp'd, Betony, Burnet, Marjoram, Mother of Thyme, Pennyroyal of each a small handful, Elder-flowers and Blessed Thistle (Carduus benedictus) a larger handful, half an ounce of Barberries bruised and one and a half ounces of Cardamums. All these ingredients are to be put in when the liquor has wrought awhile and after they are in, let it work over the vessel as little as may be when it has done work-

Elecampane ing. Fill up the cask and put into it five new-laid eggs, not broken nor crack'd. Stop it close and it will be fit to drink in two years.

John Nott 1723

Shrub

A quart of water, a pint of white wine & a quarter of a pint of Brandy, two large Lemons, pare & squese in the juice & one of ye Peeles. Put all into an earthen pot with as much fine sugar as will sweeten it to your taste. Let it stand 3 or 4 days close covered. Strain it through a jelly bagg & bottle it. It must be clear put up into ye Bottles.

BEER AND ALES

They sell good Beer at Haslemere
And under Guildford Hill.
At Little Cowfold as I've been told
A beggar may drink his fill:
There is a good brew in Amberley too,
And by the bridge also;
But the swipes they take in at Washington Inn
Is the very best Beer I know.
Hilare Belloc, West Sussex drinking song

Treacle Beer

Add to two quarts of boiling water one pound of treacle or molasses; add eight quarts of cold water and a teacup of yeast and put all into a cask until fit to drink in two or three days (or to be bottled). If the beer is to be kept, a handful of hops and another of malt are added and raisins, wormwood and spices could be included.
Susannah Stacey

Good Old English Beer

For very strong beer we use twelve bushels of malt to make a hogshead and a half. The hot water is poured on the malt in the tubs and well mashed for the first hour, then covered and left to infuse for three hours. Then the liquor is poured on to the hops (three quarters of a pound of hops to the bushel of wort). This is brought to the boil and kept boiling for two hours. A pailful is cooled, and three quarts of yeast put to it; the next day this will be strained on to the rest of the beer, which is then ready to be poured off into the casks. The bung holes are covered with paper until the beer has stopped working, then they are stopped with hops previously dried in the oven. The beer is left in the bottles for another year before it is at its best for drinking. March or April are the months for brewing and this beer will keep for ten years. It is strong beer for those who are used to it.
A countrywoman 1929

When hersdmen and shepherds got together at the big agricultural shows, renewing acquaintanceship from year to year, they celebrated in the evening, after judging, by brewing Sussex Tea. A proper brew had to made in the bucket from which the champion had been fed.

This was filled with a gallon or so of water which was boiled. Then tea – 'the biggest part of a quarter pound packet' according to shepherd John Randall – was tied in a piece of rag and plunged into the boiling water. Milk was added and a large amount of sugar was poured in and stirred.

Then the really serious business of brewing began. The head brewer, watched by the rest of the company, would, with due reverence, add the whisky. This varied from six to eight bottles according to the generosity of the champion's owner. The mixture of tea and whisky was stirred well, the bucket returned to the primus or gas ring, and the heat turned down until the mixture was gently simmering.

The simmering seemed to go on for about an hour, with the brewer sitting alongside the bucket, stirring gently. The result, apparently, was 'pure nectar, a drink to savour' but with the kick of a mule.

REMEDIES FOR EVERY ILL

PLANTS and insects, slugs and snails, frogs and frogspawn, mice and ants' eggs, crushed crawfish and cocks' combs all had their place in the country pharmacopoeia of old Sussex. In medieval times medicine was a strange mixture of astrology, superstition, herbs and blood-letting. Traditional treatments for minor ailments, and many more serious illnesses, were passed down from generation to generation. Some are still in use, such as dock leaves for nettle stings, a blue bag for wasp stings and a camphorated oil rub for a wheezy chest.

The county has always been rich in the abundance and species of its wild flowers and healing herbs. A recent survey of the area around the ruins of the Priory of St Pancras in Lewes revealed that a surprising number of the medicinal and culinary herbs planted in the monastic garden 900 years earlier were still growing in the immediate vicinity.

'There be no herb nor weed but God hath given virtue to them to help man,' wrote Andrew Boorde in his *Dietary of Health,* in which he advised on preventive medicine. His *Breviary of Health*, published five years later, in 1547, was written for physicians and surgeons.

Among his cures, one for hoarseness involved gargling to 'purge the phlegm' then drinking buttered ale or beer for three or four days. For burns, he recommended a raw egg beaten with an ounce of oil of roses, the juice of half an ounce of house leek, nightshade and plantain added.

The mixture was used to wash the wound after which a plaster of oil of roses and

The houseleek

112

plaintain juice was applied.

World War One created, for a period, a resurgence of interest in old time cures. For many years druggists had been importing herbs from Europe and further afield, but the trade ceased when war broke out and women and schoolchildren were rallied to seek out red valerian, foxglove, yarrow, dandelion, burdock, betony, wood sage, fumitory, comfrey, nightshades and many more. Again, during World War Two, the government appealed for the collection of wild plants with medicinal properties and these were gathered and dried by members of the Women's Institute.

Susannah Stacey planted an extensive herb garden at Stantons Farm. When she was asked by a Lewes doctor to make an essence of belladonna, the deadly nightshade, for lumbago plasters the distillation she obtained was declared by local doctors to be the best they had ever known.

Belladonna thrives on chalk soil and Mrs Stacey went into production on a large scale, sowing seeds at Cripps Plantation on the northern escarpment of the Downs near the farm. Over many years the plant was cultivated, harvested and made into the valuable essence until cheap imports of belladonna from Europe flooded the market and the wild garden was no longer maintained.

Many years after her death, when the First World War brought these imports to an end, a manufacturing chemist asked Mrs Stacey's son if he knew where on the Downs belladonna grew in abundance. Its essence was urgently needed by eye specialists to dilate the pupils of their patients' eyes, to simplify examination and operation. The son remembered the wild garden his mother had planted fifty years before and led the chemist there. They found the plant still flourishing and were able to harvest large supplies.

Atropa belladonna

113

Among the simples used by Mrs Stacey to cure the countryfolk who flocked to her 'clinics', many of them bringing their animals to receive attention as well, were:

An Excellent Tonic

Boil two ordinary bunches of watercress ten minutes in a pint of water; the strained water to be drunk in equal parts of milk. To each teacupful add a tablespoonful of lime water. Can be taken freely at any time.

Pill for an Aching Tooth

Take half a grain of opium, and the same quantity of yellow sub-sulphate of quicksilver, formerly called turpeth mineral; make them into a pill, and plate it in the hollow of the tooth some time before bed-time, with a small piece of wax over the top.

Remedy for a Swelled Face

Put a quarter of a pound of fresh butter into a small saucepan, over a gentle fire; and, when it begins to melt, add two tablespoonfuls of rose water, well stirring and mixing them together. Rub the part affected with this ointment, quite hot, three or four times a day, till the swelling disappears.

Stomach Plaister for Coughs

Take an ounce each of bees' wax, Burgundy pitch, and rosin; melt them together in a pipkin, and stir in three quarters of an ounce of common turpentine, and half an ounce of oil of mace. Spread it on a piece of sheep's leather, grate some nutmeg over, and apply it quite warm to the stomach.

A patent medicine widely advertised in the 1750s was Jackson's Tincture 'an effectual remedy for the Gravel, Stone, Cholick, Wind and Griping of the Guts. . . very efficacious in Coughs, Asthma and most disorders of the breath and lungs. . . an excellent medicine against spitting or vomiting blood and an immediate cure for the Piles, for Burns, Scalds, Cuts, Bruises, Green Wounds. . . It cures the toothache, cleanses, purifies and whitens the teeth, preserves the gums and sweetens the breath. . . has been found of the greatest service in dangerous disorders accidentally happening to women after lying in.' A cure-all indeed, and further it was recommended for 'the several disorders to which cattle are subject'. It cost one shilling.

More expensive, at one and sixpence a bottle, was Dr John Davis's Itch Water 'which without smell or confinement cures the Itch in all its different kinds in three or four days when all other applications have failed'.

Rowley's Herb Snuff and Tobacco was sold as a cure for blindness, Dr Boerhaave's Grand Balsam of Health was for stomach pains, purple fever, stone and gravel; Dr Coetlogon's Balsamick Vulnerary and Stiptick Tincture was for breath and lung complaints, wounds, burns, cuts and bruises 'may be kept an hundred years and carried to the remotest parts of the world without losing its virtues'; Gilbert's Sure and Certain Cure was for rheumatism.

There were dozens if not hundreds of country cures for trifling and serious complaints. For earache a shallot was baked and placed in the ear. Another treatment was to heat ash twigs until the pith ran; the liquid was then spooned into the aching ear.

Deafness was treated by taking the inside fat of an adder and hanging it on a nail on a south facing wall in the summer. A receptacle caught the drops of fat melted by the sun and a few drops of the oil were placed in the ear. The theory was that like cures like – the adder being deaf. This highly prized remedy was certainly effective in loosening wax and making hearing clearer.

A gamekeeper's remedy for adder bite was a teaspoon of salt followed by two tablespoons of olive oil and a stiff whisky.

Another early homoeopathic (like cures like) remedy was to give rabbits' brains to teething infants, or to hang a baked shrew in a bag around the child's neck. The reference is to the sharp teeth of rabbits and shrews.

Toothache was treated by a poultice of poppyhead and camomile boiled down and pulped together. The more superstitious believed that a splinter of wood from a gibbet, applied to a painful tooth, effected a cure.

Great faith was placed in red flannel, a perfectly ordinary woven wool fabric, dyed red, intended for warm underskirts. Perhaps there was something in the dye that gave it healing properties; more likely the common belief that red flannel was good for just about everything resulted from over-embroidered old wives' tales.

Onion porridge wrapped in red flannel was a common country cure for a cold, a piece of red flannel worn around the neck cured a sore throat, and a girdle of red flannel was the remedy for lumbago. A strip of red flannel folded seven times and drawn between the toes was said to cure cramp.

Warts were rubbed with beef, or an onion, after which the meat or the onion was thrown into the cesspit; as it rotted so the wart rotted. Alternatively, the sufferer could rub a snail on the wart or impale the snail on a thorn; as it shrivelled the wart vanished. In Lewes in the 1880s there was a shopkeeper in Malling Street called Janet Steer who 'cured' warts by buying them from the sufferers at a halfpenny each.

For sores an ointment was made with house leeks. The plant, called sungreen by cottagers, grew on roofs and walls, and chewing a leaf of it was the remedy for an ulcerated mouth. Sungreen on a roof was thought to save the house from a lightning strike.

Similar ointments were made by boiling cowslips in wax and simmering elderflower heads in half their weight of unsalted lard, and straining the product into jars.

Those afflicted by boils were recommended to crawl under a bramble which had grown into the soil at both ends, and a bramble leaf, moistened and applied as a plaster, was said to draw out a thorn in the finger.

Mistletoe tea was drunk to cure St Vitus's Dance, the tiny leaves below elderflower blossoms were chewed as a laxative and primroses boiled with sugar to a syrup was taken to soothe the nerves and for insomnia.

Woodlice soaked in wine were said to cure dropsy and boiled whelks and worms were used for gunshot wounds. For the common cold sugared snails were eaten. For 'a bad stomack' snayle water was advised. This is Ann Lord's receipt for the concoction:

To Make Snayle Water

Take six snayles with houses upon their backs, heate an oven very hot and put them and stir them about, there let them lye till they have done hissing, then take them out and clean them with a corse cloath, then bruise them a little in a mortar. Then take of sullandine one handfull, ye yellow of barberry barke one handfull, hartshorn half a pound, angelica, mayden haire, bittony, Mother Thyme, Hartstongue, Balme, Scabious, Egrimony, Rosemary flowers, Cowslip flowers, of each of these a good handfull. One ounce and a half of cloves bruised. All these you must put into three gallons of the strongest ale you can get. There let them steep one night. The next day distill it in a limbock. There will run three sorts of very good water. Of the first sort you may give two spoonfulls in three spoonfulls of ale, or in what you please. Of the second, three spoonfulls, of the third, four. You may take it night and morning for three daies together. If you find not got self well at the third dayes taking, you may rest a week and then take again. This water is good for the jaundice, or any distemper of wind, or an ague, and to help a bad stomack and for a consumption.

At the sore throat stage of a cold flowers of sulphur were swallowed dry, or the sufferer gargled with a mixture of sage, port, honey and vinegar – often, probably, 'accidentally' swallowed by the patient.

When the infection moved to the bronchial tubes a plaster of vinegar and whitening was placed on the chest overnight. A spoonful of honey with a pinch of nutmeg was taken to ease a cough. A drink to sweat out a cold was made by putting a spoonful of elderberry jam (perhaps with a pinch each of ginger, cinnamon and cloves) in a cup of hot water – and blackberry vinegar was another popular cold remedy.

Old countrymen considered that nothing beat a cowdung poultice for a bad leg – but it had to be fresh, and warm.

To cure a whitlow a large black slug was placed on a piece of rag

117

and stabbed all over with a needle. The whitlow was then bandaged with the rag. A less nauseating remedy was to dip a plaintain leaf in hot water and bind it on the whitlow – underside of the leaf to draw, top side to heal.

For bleeding, the wound was covered with a spider's web, or the thin membrane from inside an eggshell. Madonna lilies were grown not just for their beauty but also to make a treatment for cuts and wounds. The petals were packed down tightly in a jar of brandy and stoppered closely until the alcohol had eaten away the flesh of the petals, leaving just the skin. When needed a highly sterilised petal was peeled off and placed on the wound.

There were a number of unpleasant remedies involving snakes for goitre. One, recorded by the Rev H J Coker Egerton in 1884, involved taking a live snake and drawing it three times round the goitre, then bottling and corking the snake and burying it. As it died and shrivelled so the goitre shrivelled and disappeared.

More bizarre, the touch of a dead man's hand was thought to cure the complaint – preferably the hand of a hanged man, as he swung on the gibbet. The *Brighton Herald* reported in 1835 that two young women afflicted with goitre attended a public hanging in Horsham and pressed the still warm hand of the executed villain to their necks in the hope of a cure.

Plantain

There were also countless remedies for rheumatism, including carrying a new potato in the pocket until it turned as hard as stone, by which time it had drawn quantities of uric acid into it from the sufferer; keeping a lump of camphor in the pocket, making a poultice of crushed chickweed or bogbean.

Live frogs were swallowed whole by consumptives. Another recommendation for tubercolosis patients was to walk among sheep. In a manuscript called *Aproved Medicins and Receipts* written by Edward Austen of Burwash in 1701, and found bound in part of an old indenture, is this:

118

Surrop for a Consumtick Coff.

Take one pint of white wine and one ounce of Lickquorish powder, and one ounce of the powder of Annice Seeds, and one ounce of Sugar Candy and half an Egg shell of the powder of allicompane and a Quarter of a pound of Treacle and eight figs slitt and 1 ounces of Raysons Slitt and stoned; put all these into ye white wine in a pewter dish, then cover the dish and set it in some charcoal and make it Boyle very softly and as it boyles there will arise a Dew upon ye dish which you must wip of, and when the Dew hath done rising take it of, and put it into a Gallypot for your use and take of it night and morning. The same is used to be a certain cure.

Southey's book, *The Doctor* (1848), edited by the poet's son-in-law, the Rev John Wood Water, vicar of West Tarring, mentions Cockwater for Consumption. 'The cock being to be chased and beaten before he was killed, or else plucked alive.' And there was a special water procured by distillation from a peck of garden snails and a quart of earth worms. Extremely nasty.

Mice were considered to have excellent healing properties. A dead mouse, dried and powdered, and taken each morning for three consecutive days was a remedy for diabetes.

The eighteenth century diarist Richard Stapley had this cure for 'hooping' cough. 'Get three field mice, flaw them, draw them, and roast one of them, and let the party afflicted eat it; dry the other two in the oven until they crumble to a powder, and put a little of this powder in what the patient drinks at night, and in the morning.'

Another whooping cough cure was to pass the patient three times under the belly of a piebald horse – and yet another was to eat bread and butter given by a couple whose names were John and Joan.

Axey – the ague – was prevalent in marshy areas and many remedies were tried. One was to swallow a live spider rolled in its own cobweb. The tiny hairs of the web contain a substance similar to quinine. Another was to trap the live spider in a nutshell and hang it around the neck in a black silk bag. If these failed, the patient could

119

write the following charm on a three-cornered piece of paper which was worn around the neck until it dropped off.

Ague, ague, I thee defy,
Three days shiver
Three days shake,
Make me well for Jesus's sake.

To prevent infection when there was a putrid fever in the house, a new brick was heated, laid on an earthen dish and sprinkled with vinegar. This not only refreshed the patient, it was thought, but prevented others in the house from becoming ill. Vinegar was used in a similar way as late as the 1940s, in a Brighton house where, when one of the children contracted measles, chicken pox or another of the common childhood complaints, he or she was put to bed in a separate room which had a blanket soaked in vinegar over the door.

An unpleasant concoction was conceived by a Dr Awsitar, a follower of Dr Richard Russell who transformed the fishing village of Brighthelmstone into the fashionable seaside resort of Brighton when he promoted the sea water cure for all ailments.

In his book *Thoughts on Brighthelmston concerning Sea Bathing and Drinking Sea-Water,* he included his blood purifier: 'Take of sea-water and milk, each four ounces, put them over the fire, and when they begin to boil add a sufficiency of cremor (cream of) tartar, to turn it into whey, strain it from the curd, and, when cool, drink it'.

Camomile, which grows wild in Sussex, has for centuries had a reputation as something of a universal medicine. In Elizabethan knot gardens the paths were planted with camomile, a dense ground covering plant which, when crushed, produces a powerful apple aroma. In the grounds of Sussex country houses camomile lawns were once commonplace, and earthen seats, upholstered with camomile, were also popular. The plant is anti-inflammatory and antiseptic, it can produce a mild sedative and its infusion is useful for fever, dyspepsia and nausea.

Camomile made into a poultice was thought to cure gangrene, and it was used, too, for soothing teas and and oils.

Camomile tea

Pour one pint of boiling water on an ounce of dried flowers. When it has stood for ten minutes, strain and sweeten with sugar or honey.

Oil of Camomile

Take oyle a pint and a halfe, and three ounces of camomile flowers dryed one day after they be gathered. Then put the oyle and the flowers in a glass and stop it close and set it into the sun by the space of forty days.

This is Tudor recipe. Medicinally the oil was taken at five to fifteeen drops on sugar.

Safeguard against the Plague.

To fume your house to prevent ye plague, Take one pound of Brimstone beat it into a powder then add to it a pound of Gunpowder, beat it fine, mix them both, and put to these as much white wine vinegar as will mix them to a past, then put it up in a gallypot & every morning, lay ye quantity of a Wallnutt of it upon a hott fire shovell in ye midst of ye roome & keep all ye windows & doors shutt untill it be outt.

Arundel ms

Doctor Burgis' Plague-Preventive

Take three pints of Musquedine & boyle in it one handfull of Rue & as much sage till one pint be boyled away, then strain it & set it on ye fire againe & put therein long pepper, ginger & nutmegs of all one ounce being beaten into fine powder, then let it boyle a while, then take it off the fire, & put there into, one ounce of metridatum & two ounces of London Treakle being dissolved into a quarter of a pint of angelica water distilled out of ye leaves & so keep this same espetially above all other medesons, & if you think yrself infected with ye Plague take morning & evening in yr bed, & if you be not infected, once or twice in a week is sufficient, in any time of ye Plague next unto God, for their was never man, woman or child that drank of this but received helpe, if ye harte was not clean mortified before, & drowned with ye poyson too long before ye drink came. Tis not only good for ye Common Plague but for ye next kindred as ye sweating sickness, small pox, measells, surfitts, & ye like. This was approved of in ye late great sickness as did much good.

Arundel ms

For those venturing abroad, whether to foreign parts or just down the road is not specified, the manuscript has this advice, although what it guards against remains a mystery.

When you goe a broad chew a clove in your mouth & eate Raisons of ye sun often in ye morning or two or 3 figgs, but they will be more efectuall if broken, and you dipp them in this powder following. Take flower of Brimstone & Bole-armonick & sugar Candy a lik quantity, mix them together being beaten all fine & keep them in a little box, & of this powder you may dipp them in, & you may put a little into a glass of sack, & drink it in ye morning & fast one hour after it, then drink a draught of worm-wood Beer & eate a piece of Breaden Butter before you go abroad.

The same source gives this curious treatment for those – both people and animals – bitten by a mad dog.

Take ye leaves of Rue picked from ye stalks & bruised six ounces, garlick picked from ye stalks & bruised, Venice Treacle or Mithridate & ye scrapings of pewter, of each four ounces. Boile all these together over a slow fire in two quarts of strong ale till one pint be consumed, then keep it in a Botle close stopped, & give of it nine spoonfuls to a man or woman. Warm seven mornings fasting, & six to a Dog, to a beast 11 or 12 spoonfulls, cold to a sheep or hog, 4 spoonfulls. This ye author believes with (God's Blesings) will not fail if it be given within nine days after ye biting of ye mad dog. Apply some of ye ingredient from which ye Liquor was strained, to ye bitten place. Ye scraping of block tinn is better than pewter.

English Hypocras

For easing palpitations and tremors of the heart, removing fearful apprehensions, sudden frights, and startings, warming a cold stomach and giving rest to wearied limbs. Infuse for a few hours, in about three quarts of good white wine, a pound and a half of loaf sugar, an ounce of cinnamon, two or three tops of sweet marjoram, and a little long pepper, all slightly beaten in a mortar. Let the liquor run through a filtering bag, with a grain of musk: add the juice of a large lemon; give it gentle heat over the fire; pour it on the spices again; and when it has stood three or four days, strain it through a filtering bag and bottle it for use. This is an excellent cordial to refresh and enliven the spirits. If a red colour be wished for, the hypocras may be made of any required hue, by substituting red for white wine; or adding juice of elderberries or mulberries, syrup of clove-gilliflowers, cochineal, etc.

Inhaler

Susannah Stacey

Grand Ptisan Diet Drink

Take about a quart of best sifted and well washed oats, and a small hand-ful of wild succory roots newly drawn out of the earth; boil them gently for three quarters of an hour in six quarts of river water, and then add half an ounce of crystal-mineral, and a quarter of a pound of the best honey. Let the whole boil half an hour longer; strain it through linen, put the liquid in an earthen vessel, and leave it covered to cool. For persons of bilious habit, use only half the quantity of honey, as the sweetness has a tendency to increase the bile. Two good glasses of this ptisan should be drunk every morning fasting, without eating anything for some hours; and the same quantity three hours after dinner. This course must be continued for four-teen days, without bleeding or confinement, or any particular diet, but liv-ing in all respects as usual.

Susannah Stacey

There were cures, too, for physical defects, like freckles, baldness and wrinkles. One recommended those with freckles to 'take the bloud of a hare & the bloud of a bull & annoynt the face therewith' or, if the sufferer were less than sanguine, to take 'a new laid Egg, lay it in as much wine vinegar as will cover it, let it lay in it til the shel be eat off, then wash the liquor when you go to bed'. An 'exce-lent face water' was made with six quarts of new milk and fifty live crawfish pounded in a pestle and mortar.

Then, as now, there were endless cures for baldness; one involved mixing half an ounce of myrhh in a pint of sack and washing the head with it. Another consisted of baked nutmegs beaten up with salad oil and honey water. A third read: 'Garden snails to be plucked out of their houses and pounded with horse-leeches, bees, wasps and salt, an equal quantity of each; and the baldness. . . to be anointed with the moisture from this mixture after it had been buried eight days in a hot bed'.

Paste for chapped hands

Mix a quarter of a pound of unsalted hog's lard, which has been washed in water and then rose water, with the yolks of two new laid eggs, and a large spoonful of honey. Add as much fine oatmeal, or almond paste, as will work it into a paste.

A substance to take out superfluous hairs was made by mixing two and a half ounces of rosin with an ounce of beeswax and forming it into sticks. For shiny, healthy hair, a rinse was made by steeping one pound of rosemary leaves in boiling water. After twelve hours the water was strained and half an ounce of Jamaica rum was added to it.

Ann Lord's remedy for removing 'ffreckles of the fface' was 'wash your fface in ye wane of the moon with a sponge morning and evening with ye distilled water of elder leaves letting ye same dry into the skin. Your water must be distilled in May.'

Superstition was still rife in the early years of the twentieth century. During an outbreak of diphtheria in the 1930s Lewes mothers were taking their children to a wise woman in Malling Street who tied a hazel twig to their throat, charged them a shilling and, if that failed to effect a cure, made the children swallow stewed mice – the cost being half a crown.

FOOD IN WARTIME

The ingenuity of housewives was taxed to a greater extent during World War Two than had their mothers' been a generation earlier. By 1939 fewer families grew their own vegetables and the women had become accustomed to buying conveniently packaged and canned goods.

'How little thought we, who saw the last war from a schoolroom, ever gave to the cheapness and abundance of such commodities as sugar,' wrote Marjorie Hassell Tiltman. 'In time of peace you had your garden as you liked. If you preferred to have it all flowers and buy your vegetables, that was your affair,' said author Anthony Armstrong. 'In time of war however, it was not; it was part of your country, a small island of only 90,000 square miles. To grow as many of your own vegetables was then duty.'

Hilda Chamberlain, sister of the Prime Minister, Neville Chamberlain, addressing assembled delegates of West Sussex Women's Institutes, urged everyone who could to keep poultry. Every village, she said, should have a poultry club and if everyone who had a garden had a fowl run in it, this would make an important contribution to the national cause.

Likewise, the Ministry of Food urged larger households – where there was likely to be more in the way of table scraps – to keep a pig. This was a suggestion harking back two or three generations to when all but the poorest cottager kept a pig in the back garden.

So the women, children, older men and those in reserved occupations, dug for victory, turning over their gardens to the wholesale production of food. But what were they to do with the surplus produce?

Jam was one way of preserving fruit, if the government released some sugar for the purpose; or it could be bottled, using ordinary jam jars with waxed paper covers if vacuum jars were unobtainable. Some fruit was suitable for preserving in Campden solution, other types could be dried.

Dried Apple Rings

Wipe the apples, remove the cores and peel thinly. Cut out any blemishes. Slice into thin rings. Steep the rings for ten minutes in water containing one and a half ounces of salt to the gallon. Thread the rings on sticks or canes to fit across the oven or spread on trays. Dry very slowly until they feel like chamois leather. Turn once or twice during cooking. Pears can be treated in the same way, but they must be cut in halves or quarters and spread on the trays.

Vegetables, too, could be dried and bottled, and all types of beans could be salted down in jars.The decorative garden, where it remained, also contributed to the war effort between 1939 and 1945. Dead heading the roses, essential for continuous blooms, became a thing of the past because rose hips were in demand for rose hip syrup. The hips were harvested, taken to the local chemist and sold.

Those without the time, the facilities or the basic skill to preserve their own produce could take fruit and vegetables to the small canning plants set up by Women's Institutes in church halls and village halls. They paid fivepence for each can.

In the first year of the war the government allowed an unexpected bonus of sugar for jam makers, and in some Sussex villages there was a co-operative effort with the WI taking charge of all the locally grown fruit and making all the jam. In 1941 the rules changed and the government proposed local jam pools with everyone who contributed fruit or voluntary help being eligible for ten pounds of jam at wholesale price. The fruit growers were not pleased, and less so when the rules changed again and all the jam went to the local shop where it was sold back to the producers and jam makers at the rate of one pound of jam per head per month.

Rationing was quite stringent. Typically, in 1940, one person was permitted each week four ounces of bacon or ham, eight ounces of sugar, two ounces of tea, about two shillings' worth of meat, an ounce of cheese, four ounces of butter, two ounces of cooking fats or margarine. Jam, marmalade, treacle and syrup were not rationed until March, 1941 and later that year the distribution of dried milk was controlled, with National Dried Milk introduced in December. Points were needed to buy it. Whalemeat and snoek arrived in the fishmongers' in 1945.

Shortages of food, fuel and staff in World War Two made a passable cook of novelist Sheila Kaye-Smith, who until then had never made a cup of tea nor boiled and egg. Learning as she went along she devised her own recipes in accordance with rationing. Soup, she said, need not be simmered for hours – it could be done in an hour to save fuel. Here is her recipe:

Save Fuel Soup

Two large potatoes, three medium onions, small stick of celery, a pint of water and a pint of milk (or you can use Household Milk). Small piece of margarine, a tablespoonful of flour, pepper and salt. Grate the potatoes and onions on the large side of the grater. This is a good way out of the usual dainty dicing, which takes more time, more trouble and more fuel. Melt your margarine in the saucepan. When it is making the sizzling noise which shows it is ready for cooking, put in the vegetables and put on the saucepan lid. Make sure that the heat is very low. Shake the saucepan from time to time and after ten minutes pour on the water, hot or cold, and seasoning and turn up the heat a little, but do not let the soup cook fast. Simmer until the vegetables are quite soft, about twenty minutes. Make a paste of the flour and a little milk. Add gradually to the soup over a low heat, then add the rest of the milk. Turn up the heat and stir with a wooden spoon until the soup is thick and boiling. You can vary the recipe by adding bacon rind to the vegetables at the start, or two tablespoons of grated cheese at the finish.